© THE BAKER & TAYLOR CO.

Your Energy-Efficient Home

Floyd Hickok is a former technical writer, having spent over a quarter of a century as an electronics writer and as a manager of publications departments in industry. During this period he wrote dozens of books having to do with complex radar, satellite trackers, computers, and so on. When the energy crisis hit, he asked himself, "What can I do?" and he decided that he could write about energy. Since then Mr. Hickok has written *Handbook of Solar and Wind Energy, The Buy Wise Guide to Solar Heat,* and has contributed to *Solar Energy Digest* and *Solar Age.*

Your Energy-Efficient Home

IMPROVEMENTS TO SAVE UTILITY DOLLARS

Floyd Hickok

AN HOUR HOUSE BOOK

A SPECTRUM BOOK

Prentice-Hall, Inc., Englewood Cliffs, New Jersey 07632

Library of Congress Cataloging in Publication Data

HICKOK, FLOYD
   Your energy-efficient home.

   (A Spectrum Book)
   First published in 1977 under title: Home improve-
ments for conservation and solar energy.
   "An Hour House book."
   Bibliography: p.
   Includes index.
   1. Dwellings—Insulation. 2. Solar heating.
3. Dwellings—Energy conservation. I. Title.
TH1715.H5 1979   693.8'32   78-26506
ISBN 0-13-978312-1
ISBN 0-13-978304-0 pbk.

A SPECTRUM BOOK

Printed in the United States of America

10 9 8 7 6 5 4 3 2 1

The equations and data for hourly heat loss calculation and solar inputs are from
ASHRAE literature and are used with their permission. The illustrations on pages 33,
39, 46, 76, 84, 94, and 97, showing the use of insulation and the effect of the sun on
buildings, are furnished courtesy of Owens-Corning Fiberglas Corporation. Drawings
on page 4 courtesy of Dynamic Graphics, Inc.

Editorial/production supervision and interior design by Maria Carella
Cover design by Tony Ferrara Studio
Cover illustration by Mona Mark
Manufacturing buyer: Cathie Lenard

PRENTICE-HALL INTERNATIONAL, INC., *London*
PRENTICE-HALL OF AUSTRALIA, PTY., LIMITED, *Sydney*
PRENTICE-HALL OF CANADA, LTD., *Toronto*
PRENTICE-HALL OF INDIA PRIVATE, LIMITED, *New Delhi*
PRENTICE-HALL OF JAPAN, INC., *Tokyo*
PRENTICE-HALL OF SOUTHEAST ASIA PTE., LTD., *Singapore*
WHITEHALL BOOKS, LIMITED, *Wellington, New Zealand*

Dedicated to all the little people who are helping us to help ourselves. Grateful acknowledgments are also extended to Audrey Merrill, for editorial assistance, and to Dr. William A. Shurcliff, for technical review.

Preface

One of the fundamental laws of nature says that heat moves from a hot body to a cold body until they are both the same temperature. That's why the inside of the house gets cold in winter. The hot inside tries to reach an equilibrium with the cold outside. Since the outside is so much bigger than the inside, the house gets as cold as the outside, unless some heat is added to the inside.

There's nothing you can do about it, except slow up the escape of the inside warmth. If you are building a new home, you can make the rate of escape very slow. You can make it so tight that the heat of the appliances and the people add warmth about as fast as it escapes.

Such a super-tight house would be pretty hard to build. Instead, you can build a very tight house and build it in such a way that the sun can add a great deal more heat to the inside than it does in most homes. Now, with the people and the appliances and the solar gain, the home stays warm even on rather cold days.

If you are building a new home, you can plan it and build it in such a way that these "passive" sources add heat about as fast as heat escapes. But can you do anything about the established home in which you now live to make it like this new super energy-efficient home?

Some of the experts say it can't be done. Theoretically and practically the experts are wrong. However, no one has ever done it, actually, because no one has ever said to himself, "I'll bet I can do it." Upgrading a home to this new level of energy efficiency remains a challenge.

FLOYD HICKOK
Scituate, Massachusetts

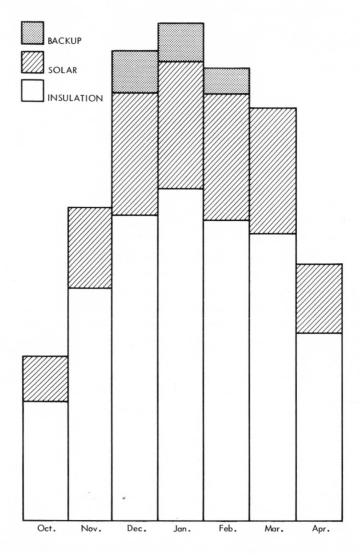

The average American home could become almost independent of fuel for heat. The dark grey bars show the relative amount of fuel that would be needed, the light grey bars show the solar input, and the white bars show the fuel that would NOT be spent—if the home were completely upgraded. Truly, insulation is the best "black gold" around.

Contents

1

Learning
About Heat

There's a new reason for remodeling. At one time you spent money fixing up the old place if you needed more room, or if you wanted to modernize or if you wanted to improve its appearance. Now you can have a new motivation. The new reason for remodeling is that it can solve the crisis between comfort and the fuel bill.

The past few seasons have wreaked havoc on our heating budget, and there's no change in sight, except things will get worse. Our helpless frustration leads us to despair.

But despair is the worst possible response to the situation. What we must do now is think, inquire, study, learn and plan. Then we must act before the high cost of fuel depletes our personal resources so badly we have nothing left to work with.

Instead of being frightened by the high fuel bills, let us be guided by this thought: with the right course of action we can keep our home comfortable and still spend less on fuel. Should we set the thermostat back to 68, or even 65, to save fuel? It is the poorest recourse in the world when alternatives are available.

Whenever a group of consumers attend an energy information meeting the question very quickly gets around to the subject of comfort. Suppose we do go to another heat source, such as solar energy. Can the sun keep us warm in winter? It seems inconceivable. In mid-winter the sun may shine brightly, but the weather is still cold. How, then, can solar heat be trusted to keep us comfortable? Especially since the sun shines only a small part of the time we need it. The question involves not so much whether solar heat will work—it obviously does—but whether it works well enough to keep us comfortable.

Those with economists' minds, who assume that all motivation is in terms of money, say that the cost of changing to a different energy source in the home is what concerns people most. We suggest that the desire for comfort is just as strong a motivation. If we have a strong enough desire to be comfortable, we will find some change of energy system that will be within our range of ability to pay.

Should Comfort Be the Criterion?

The energy crisis frustrates our desire for comfort. Since we say that the first steps in combating frustration are to think, inquire, study, learn and plan, we say that we should look at comfort and find out what it means to us.

The interest in conservation and solar energy has attracted a great many back-to-nature enthusiasts. These folks tend to think that a constant 70 degrees is not necessarily the best way to live. We hear them making such remarks as: Temperature swings of 10 or even 20 degrees inside a house is not only bearable but healthy; in the millions of years before housing the human body became geared to withstand large swings of temperature; in fact, the body needs the swings of temperature to stay healthy; the constant incubation in houses of even temperature may account for much of human ill health and insecurity.

Most people disagree with these comments. Some people feel a lessened feeling of well-being at temperatures below 70. Many people feel a greatly reduced capacity to perform work when the temperature is below a rather constant 72 to 74 degrees. There are others, of course, who come into a 68 degree office and immediately throw open the window even on a cold winter day. The desired temperature varies widely among individuals, but there seems to be for each person some rather fixed range of temperature for optimum comfort and function. We suggest that the maintenance of some rather constant temperature is indeed of great benefit. Nature found out long ago that in order to evolve more competent species body temperature had to be regulated to a warm and very precise constant temperature level.

We are therefore going to follow the premise that discovery of a way to maintain a precise, constant temperature is as important a step in the progress of civilization as it was to the evolvement of life on earth. Without having discovered how to be warm-blooded creatures, animals would not have evolved beyond the lizard stage. We may say of the fossil fuel age that it taught us the value and techniques of maintaining a constant temperature in the living space. We say that, as we switch to renewable energy sources, the technology of maintaining a constant temperature must follow along with the new methods.

Unfortunately we shall not be able to settle the dispute between the Eskimos and the Arabs over whether the constant temperature should be 68, 70, 72 or 74 degrees. These individual preferences are as much a part of individual metabolism as the heart beat and blood pressure. Wherever there are two or more people occupying the same living space there will be disputes over the level of constant temperature. If technology could contrive a means whereby each person could surround himself with his own preferred temperature, we might have another great step in progress. What we shall settle for here is the assumption that the living space should have a constant temperature of 70 degrees during the waking hours.

Note in passing that it is not practical to maintain an absolute temperature in the home. Thermostats can be built to respond to very small changes in temperature, but precision models are too expensive for the home. Anyway, if the thermostat could respond to a fraction of a degree of temperature change, the heat source would have to come on and go off every minute or so—not a very sensible way to run a heating system. The only practical answer is to allow the temperature to swing a degree or two above and below the set point before the thermostat acts.

HEAT MOTION

Heat flows in only one direction—from hot to cold. If you think about it long enough and hard enough you will discover that this simple fact is one of the most profound characteristics of the universe. There are a few other one-way streets in the universe, too, such as the fact that water will always run down hill. These one-way movements are called irreversible processes. Nature has some reversible processes, too. As soon as you burn a piece of wood some of it turns into carbon dioxide, which is then used by a tree to make more wood. With irreversible processes there is no way to stop the movement except with the application of energy. You can raise a fallen stone by applying energy to lift it, or raise the downstream water by applying energy to a pump, or raise the temperature of a room by applying heat energy. Left to its own devices with no interference from applied energy, heat will inexorably become colder.

You can stop water from running down hill by putting up a dam, and you can stop heat from flowing by putting up a dam, which is called insulation. However, there is a difference between the flow of water and the flow of heat. We can stop the flow of water completely, but we cannot stop heat flow completely. Insulation, or the heat dam, provides "resistance" to the heat flow, but resistance does not block all heat flow. The more insulation, the more resistance to heat flow, but we cannot add enough insulation to stop all of it.

HEAT IDEAS

Most of us learned some place along the line that heat moves in three ways—by radiation, convection and conduction. At the time we learned it most of us probably thought, "So what. That doesn't mean anything to me. I'll never use it." Now, confronted with the heat crisis, we'd better know what it means! We must learn how to make use of this knowledge, if we want to be comfortable. Let's refresh our memories.

We do not need to understand involved technical ideas to realize what heat radiation is. Each time we bask in the warm glow of the heat from a fireplace we know about heat radiation. What we must come to realize now is that heat is always escaping from any surface by radiation. A lot of heat radiates from the glowing coals in the fireplace, but a little bit is always radiating from any surface at any temperature. It's just that the hotter the surface the more radiation there is.

Heat radiation is like light radiation; they are both wavelengths of energy. The big difference is in the wavelength. Heat radiation has a longer wavelength than light. Remember that light rays cannot be bent, but they can be blocked by an opaque material, and they can be reflected by shiny material. Heat radiation, being a wavelength, behaves the same way. It can be blocked by a material opaque to these longer wavelengths, and it can be reflected. Insulation against heat transfer by radiation is fairly easy to apply. We need only to put up a material opaque to heat (or "infrared") or capable of reflecting the escaping radiation back into the room.

Heat also escapes from a surface by convection. Convection means to carry away. There has to be a moveable fluid such as air in contact with a surface for convection to occur. When an air molecule touches a hot surface, it absorbs a little bit of the heat and then moves away carrying that tiny bit of heat with it. When millions of molecules carry away a little bit of heat every minute, it soon adds up to a great deal of heat.

The way to keep heat from escaping by convection is to keep air (or other fluids) from touching the hot surface. The only real way to do it is to put the surface in a vacuum. The people who make thermos bottles can do it, but the people who build houses cannot. No doubt many inventors have dreamed of putting a vacuum between the inner and outer skins of a house, but the practical solution eludes them.

Lacking a vacuum, the next best thing is to prevent the movement of air molecules as much as possible. If the molecules cannot move away

7

from the surface, they cannot carry the heat away. Still air is a better "insulator" than moving air (e.g., wind) because the air molecules cannot carry the heat away so fast.

If you can avoid warming up a surface, such as the outside skin of a house, very little heat will escape by either radiation or convection.

There is a very insidious kind of convection that can raise havoc with your heating bill. It is called "infiltration." The term refers to the cold air that gets into your home from cracks, tiny holes and open doors. A hole no larger than a pencil diameter can cost you many dollars over the heating season.

Heat also escapes by conduction, or passing through a material. If one molecule in a substance gets warm, the molecule next to it soaks up some of that heat and becomes warm, too. Then the next one and the next one and the next one gets warm. Heat gets through a material by conduction just as bucket of water moves along a line in a bucket brigade.

There is just no way we can keep heat from going by conduction through a material such as a wall. There is no way we can keep one molecule from touching one other in a solid. Remember, heat always goes from hot to cold, so it always goes from a warmer molecule to a cooler one. There's no way to stop the flow. How, then, does insulation keep heat in a house?

The answer is, although heat inevitably moves from hot to cold, it takes some time to get there. Heat does not travel with great speed down a length of molecules the way electricity does. When we put electrical energy into a pair of wires connected to a light bulb 100 miles away, the bulb glows almost instantly. Not so with heat by conduction. It moves rather slowly.

Heat also moves by conduction at different speeds in different materials. Some of us have discovered by our pain that if we hold a piece of metal and heat one end, the place where our hand is gets hot very quickly. But we can take a dish out of a hot oven by grasping it with a cloth in our hand. Heat moves rapidly through metal but slowly through other materials such as cloth.

The walls of our home keep the heat in because they are of a material through which conducted heat moves very slowly. In fact, builders select wall material partly on the basis of its poor heat conductance, and then they increase the resistance to heat transfer by adding insulation.

The thickness of the wall influences how long it will take for heat to escape from a room by conduction. If a room drops 10 degrees in an hour with a 1″ wall, it will take 5 hours for it to drop 10 degrees if the wall is 5 inches thick. We could feel comfortable in a room with very little heat added if we had walls many inches thick and if they were made of poor conducting material.

While radiation, convection and conduction are the three important properties of heat relating to our comfort, there are still other important ideas about heat to keep in mind. One is equilibrium temperature. If we place two stones, one rather cold and the other rather hot, into an insulated box, we will discover after a while that both stones (and the air and interior walls of the box) have become the same temperature, which will be a little less than the hot stone and a little more than the cold stone. Heat from the hot stone has passed to the cold stone until they are both the same temperature. After equilibrium temperature has been reached, no further change occurs.

Our own body, by maintaining temperature equilibrium, gives us a sense of comfort. Our metabolic processes keep our body temperature at 98 degrees. We must dissipate some heat in order to maintain the 98 degrees. The comfortable environment is one where the body can lose just enough heat to maintain temperature without shivering or sweating. If the air and the walls and the furniture in the room are between 70 and 78 degrees, the body, for most people, maintains its equilibrium between its own heat loss and the capacity of the surroundings to absorb heat.

We sense what this heat balance means when we sit next to a cold wall in a comfortable room. The side of our body next to the wall feels cold. On that side the body transfers more heat by radiation and convection to the wall than it does to the rest of the room.

The body's reaction to heat balance explains why it is possible in some homes to feel chilly even when the air temperature inside is 75 degrees. If the house is poorly insulated, the heat is escaping at a fairly rapid rate. Heat escapes from the body at the same rate, and discomfort results. We thus see the benefits of insulation. If the home is so well insulated that very little heat escapes, our bodies do not lose heat so rapidly, and we feel comfortable at temperatures less than 75 degrees. Good insulation requires less heat input to make us feel comfortable.

Another important property of heat is the fact that heat rises. The air at the ceiling is warmer than the air at the floor. This property has more to do with management of heat than with comfort. We should keep this property in mind because, if it is mismanaged, it can cause discomfort. Also, there are ways to make use of this property in the distribution of heat.

Relative humidity, while not a heat property, has an important bearing on our comfort. For those who have forgotten what relative humidity means, it refers to a mathematical figure which expresses the ratio between the amount of water vapor actually in the air and the amount that the air could contain at that temperature. When air has absorbed all the water vapor it can, it is said to be saturated. If the air is below saturation, it readily takes up water vapor. Humidity is a function of temperature. The warmer the air, the greater the amount of water vapor it can hold before saturation.

If we are in a 70 degree room and the air is very dry, the perspiration on our skins evaporates rapidly, and we feel chilly. If the air is at an adequate relative humidity, evaporation of perspiration is slow, and we feel comfortable.

We should also keep in mind that it takes a certain amount of energy to evaporate water to bring it to the desired level if the relative humidity is low.

Infiltration can increase the discomfort caused by low relative humidity. In winter the outside cold air is usually quite dry. At least, whatever its dryness, when this cold air becomes warm its relative humidity is much less because the warmer air could hold a lot more moisture than it had when cold. If outside cold air gets in the house by infiltration, its relative humidity drops when it warms up in the house. Blocking infiltration has a double benefit. Less heat input is required because there is less cold air to warm up, and the comfort level can be at a lower temperature.

We will next expand on these ideas about heat so as to show how to cut down on heat loss, or reduce fuel bills, and to show how remodeling can be combined with heat loss reduction. We suggest that every remodeling job undertaken nowadays be considered on the basis of its ability to increase the energy efficiency of your home. We suggest that any home improvement or remodeling not capable of upgrading the energy efficiency of your home should have a low priority. A firm that does retrofit design: Hawkweed Group, 4643 North Clark St., Chicago, IL 60640.

2

Being
Your Own
Engineer

You could, if you wished, call in a heating engineer who would redesign your home for maximum energy efficiency. This route would cost you a lot of money.

Let's see how you could do some of the basic engineering yourself. It's not that hard. All it requires is that you learn some elemental facts and procedures about the behavior of heat in a house. The facts and procedures are easy to learn. In the coming age of energy crises the future will belong to those who become knowledgeable. Survival with dignity will go to those who base their choices on knowledge.

The engineering math you will encounter will consist of easy equations. If you can handle arithmetic, you can handle these equations. Sometimes these equations involve a lot a of numbers, so the best tool you can have is a hand calculator.

On the question of numbers, you may at first be upset by the large amount of numbers you will find in this book. What we have done is work out some of the problems for you, so all you have to do is adapt the answers to your own situation. We get a lot of numbers when we work out answers for a lot of situations. We tabulate these answers in charts. In these charts you will be interested in one, or perhaps two or three, numbers. So there may be a lot of numbers, but you will be concerned about very few of the total.

BASIC FACTS

Since you will be dealing with quantitative measures of real physical properties in these equations, you must learn what some of these quantities are. We list below the definitions of these properties. You need to remember what these properties mean.

British Thermal Unit (Symbol: Btu)

This term is the unit quantity of heat that is used in most energy problems today. It is defined as the amount of heat required to raise one pound of water one degree Fahrenheit. When the country goes metric we'll have to use a different unit, but the basic idea will remain the same. An "amount of heat" is something of a figment of the imagination because there is no way to sense it the way there is in feeling the weight of a stone. But all engineering ideas have to be worked out in units. So what we do is measure the effect of this imaginary thing upon a unit of substance. What we do is take a unit of water, apply heat to it and then say that when the water rises one degree then one Btu has been added to the water. The term then becomes meaningful in everyday experience if we keep track of the amount of fuel we burned while raising the water one degree.

Millions of Btu's (Symbol: MBTU)

The Btu is a very small quantity when we come to think about the amount of heat required for a home. We will be dealing with millions of Btu's, so we find it convenient to use the special term MBTU. You will need to get used to expressing Btu's in decimal fractions of MBTU. For example, 490,000 Btu is the same as .49 MBTU.

Btu's per Hour (Symbol: Btuh)

We very frequently want to think about the amount of heat lost or added in a unit of time, one hour. In this case, instead of writing out "Btu per hour" each time we find it more convenient to write Btuh.

U Value (Symbol: U)

We emphasized in Chapter 1 that heat flows from hot to cold, and it flows at a certain rate. The standard way to think about it is to ask, "How much heat gets from here to there in one hour?" We call the number that defines this rate the "U value." There is a specific definition for U value. You need to become very familiar with this definition.

The U value is the coefficient of heat transmission. It is defined as the amount of heat per hour, expressed in Btu, moving through a square foot of surface of a material where there is one degree temperature difference between the two surface facings. Note the three factors: one square foot of surface, one hour, one degree temperature difference. If one square foot of a material transmits one Btu per hour when there is a temperature difference of one degree between the two surfaces, the material has a U value of 1. All materials have some characteristic U value.

Conductance (Symbol: C)

When you read material outside this book, you may run into the "conductance," and it may be confusing because it sounds very much like U value. It is defined as the rate of flow in Btu per hour per square foot of surface per degree difference per inch of thickness. That is, conductance is a general value referring to the heat transmission characteristic of a material per unit of thickness.

Surface Conductance (Symbol: f)

This term refers to the rate of heat transfer by radiation, convection and conduction between the surface of a material and its surroundings, usually air, expressed in Btu per hour per square foot of surface per degree temperature difference. When figuring the total heat transmission of a wall from inside to outside, surface conductance of the inside and outside become an important pair of factors. Surface conductance is greatly increased by wind because convection is increased, enabling heat transfer to take place more rapidly. For this reason, the outside of a wall has a much greater surface conductance than the inside. Outside surface conductance is greater in winter than in summer because the average wind velocity is usually higher. Engineering designers usually assume, as a design average, that the winter winds are 15 mph and the summer winds 7 1/2 mph. You will discover later how these differences are expressed in Btu.

Resistance (Symbol: R)

Mathematically it is not possible to add a series of U values and have the answer equal the total U value. You must add the reciprocals of the U values and then take the reciprocal of the answer to get the total U value. A reciprocal is the opposite of the original value. The opposite meaning of conduction is resistance. Therefore a material can have a conductance or a resistance, depending on how you want to look at it. The resistance notion is so convenient that engineers often find it better to speak of "R value." Thus, if one insulation has an R value of 4 and a second has an R value of 8, the second is twice as effective as the first.

A reciprocal is expressed mathematically as 1/N. That is, 1 divided by the number. If we have a material with a U value of .25, its R value is 1/.25 or 4. The U, C or f values can each be converted to R values by taking the reciprocal. This fact is very handy because it enables us to pull a number of characteristics together. Thus, if we know C and f we can find U with this equation:

$$U = 1/C + 1/f.$$

When you begin to compute reciprocals, you realize how valuable the hand calculator is. If a U value is .37, it is rather laborious to divide 1 by .37.

Degree Days (Symbol: DD)

When the concept of degree days first began to develop, several experimenters looked into the question, What is the outside temperature at which most people turn on their heating system? The general consensus was 65 degrees. This temperature was then taken as the base for defining degree days. If you take the highest and lowest temperature for a 24-hour

Degree Day Map

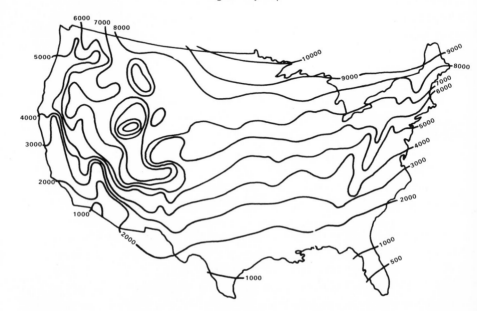

day and take the mid-point, you have the mean temperature for the day. If you subtract this mean temperature from 65, you have the degree day. For example, if the lowest is 10 and the highest is 40, the mid-point is 25 and the DD is $65 - 25 = 40$. What this number means is that the average temperature over the 24-hour day is 40 degrees. The interior temperature control system acts as though it always sees an outside temperature of 40 degrees during the 24-hour period.

Seasonal Degree Days
(Symbol: DD or SDD)

One of the most useful numbers you can have in dealing with heating problems is the seasonal degree day. This number is obtained by adding all of the daily degree days for a season.

There are three kinds of seasonal degree days of special interest to us. They are: annual DD, which is the total DD for all the months of the year; heating season DD, which, for most regions, runs from October through April; monthly DD. If you do much reading beyond this book, you will run into tables of annual DD for major cities. In this book we are sometimes going to act as though the annual and the heating season DD were the same value. This assumption is valid because the kind of generalizations we are doing here can be only approximations anyway.

In order to do your own engineering you must know your own annual heating season and monthly DD. One of your first projects should be to locate this information. It can be obtained from your local weather bureau, your oil dealer or your newspaper.

Transmission Loss (Symbol: XL)

This term refers to the transfer of heat from the inside of a building to the colder outside through the building skin, usually by means of conduction. It is expressed in Btu or Btuh. It includes the losses due to surface conductance.

Infiltration Loss (Symbol: IL)

This term refers to the energy that must be expended in bringing up to comfort temperature the cold air that gets into the house by infiltration. Every tiny crack and hole is an opportunity for cold air infiltration. In a leaky house infiltration can account for more than half the heat loss. Infiltration occurs because of pressure differences between outside and inside. There are two causes, wind and temperature differences. The higher the wind the greater the infiltration. Since the wind blows on only one side of the house at a time, the opposite side has little or no infiltration from the wind. Temperature infiltration occurs because there is a pressure difference between warm and cold air. This condition sets up what is called the "chimney effect" in a building. Cold air comes in at cracks and holes in the lower region, and warm air exits from cracks and holes in the upper region. While the chimney effect is particularly serious in tall buildings, it is also something to consider in homes.

Heat Gain (Symbol: HG)

A home is not entirely a heat dissipator. It is also a solar collector, and for that reason a home brings heat into a home. Those of us who live in an uninsulated home in the summer can vouch for that fact. But the home also collects heat in the winter from the sun, and that heat gain should be subtracted from the heat loss in order to obtain the heat load of the home.

There is some heat gain from the occupants and the appliances in a building. For most considerations we are going to ignore this source of heat gain.

Design Temperature

Winter design temperature is the average lowest temperature in a locality. The design engineer specifies a heating system capable of handling the heat load on the design temperature day. The transmission loss equation is:

$$XL = A \times U = (t_i - t_o) \text{ or}$$
$$XL = A \times U \times Td$$

A = area of a building section surface

U = transmission coefficient

$(t_i - t_o)$ = the difference temperature between the warm side and the cold side of a section. Usually, inside temperature, t_i, means the normal thermostat setting and the outside temperature, t_o, means the design temperature. However, you can make them mean any difference temperature you wish.

Td = temperature difference between two sides of a section. It means the same thing as $(t_i - t_o)$. As long as we can keep in mind that we get Td by subtracting the two temperatures we can avoid the tedious longer form. We are interested in the number of degrees that must be made up by the furnace, and that is what Td tells us.

This equation says that one square foot of building section will transfer one Btu per hour for each degree of temperature difference between inside and outside. The term "per hour" is inherent because "U" means a quantity per hour. If you want to know the transmission loss characteristics of a building section, you set A = 1 and Td = 1. If you want to know the total loss of a wall, window, floor or ceiling, you must have determined the U value of the section. This equation determines what is known as the "instantaneous" rate of heat transfer. At some one instant the transfer occurs at a determined rate, and, if it continues at that rate for an hour, the indicated Btu's will be transferred. Engineers recognize that this equation is fallacious in the real world because temperatures are always changing. However, taking the average over an hour yields a very close approximation. The infiltration loss equation is:

$$IL = V \times (t_i - t_o) \times .018 \text{ or}$$
$$IL = V \times Td \times .018$$

V = volume of air entering a building per hour. Most homes experience a complete air change once or twice every hour. A home of 10,000 cubic feet with one air change per hour will bring in 10,000 cubic feet of air from the outside each hour. Since this air must be heated, infiltration constitutes a heat expenditure, or heat loss.

$(t_i - t_o)$ = the same temperature difference encountered above.

Td is also the same temperature difference as above

.018 = a constant derived from the specific heat and density of air. Specific heat is a term that refers to the amount of heat gained by a substance relative to the same mass of water. Since the heat gain of water is expressed in Btu per unit per degree, another substance will gain a relative Btu per unit per degree. In heat engineering work the relative gain of air is taken at .018 Btu per cubic foot per degree. You see that .018 corresponds to U value because it symbolizes the rate of heat transfer per unit per degree.

Heat Loss (Symbol: HL. HL = XL + IL)

Total heat loss per hour is the sum of the transmission and infiltration losses. The total heat loss for an entire building is the sum of the heat losses of all the sections. If we want to distinguish between a building heat loss and a section heat loss we may use the symbol "HLB."

In some cases we want to know the heat loss "Q" for an entire day.

We then multiply the building heat loss by 24 (hours) and by the fraction DD/65. The equation for daily heat loss then becomes,

$$Q = (XL + IL) \times 24 \times DD/65.$$

In real life we encounter the fact that most of us set back the thermostat at night. Our Td at night may be different from our Td during daylight hours. We could compute XL and IL for both night and day, but it is simpler to use an adjustment factor. We find that, if we set back the thermostat at night to about 60, the heat loss for the entire 24 hours will be about 95% of what it would be if we kept the thermostat constant all the time—in most regions. We therefore multiply our total daily heat loss by .95 to get a truer picture. We call this quantity the adjusted QA. Then,

$$QA = (XL + IL) \times 24 \times .95 \times DD/65.$$

Seasonal Heat Loss

The ultimate number that we are interested in is the heat loss of our home for an entire season. The equation for seasonal heat loss is

$$QA = (XL + IL) \times 24 \times .95 \times SDD/65.$$

You will notice that this equation is the same as the one for daily heat loss, except that now we use seasonal degree days. You should carefully note the function of DD/65 and SDD/65 in these two equations. Remember that to compute XL we multiply AU by Td. Remember that Td is the difference between the inside and the outside average low, or design temperature. If the average low for the winter is 0 and the thermostat rests at 70, Td is 70. If the area is 1000 square feet and the U value is .25,

$$1000 \times .25 \times 70 = 17,500.$$

This 17,500 Btu per hour is the heat loss. The designer must provide a heat source capable of producing at least that amount of heat gain.

However, Td is only 70 on rare occasions, perhaps half a dozen times a year. Most of the time the heat loss is a fractional part of the worst case. How do we determine this fractional part?

Remember that, according to degree day theory, the inside of the house can stay at 70 as long as the outside weather does not go below 65. Then, when the weather is 0 degrees, the degree day temperature difference is 65. There is no fractional part to reduce XL. We can say that the fractional part is 65/65. So,

$$XL = AUTd \times 1.$$

On the other hand, if the weather is at 65, the DD is 0, and XL multiplied by 0 is 0. If the weather is at an intermediate point we have a real fraction. For example, if the weather is at 25, the difference with 65 is 40. The fraction is 40/65, and the heat loss is 40/65 of the loss at a design temperature interval.

Note that the numerator we obtain in this fraction is the same value we obtain when we derive the DD. Hence, we say that the fractional part of the worst case heat loss is DD/65.

Now remember that heat losses XL and IL are in Btuh, whereas DD has a basis in the 24-hour day. We must convert the heat loss into Btu per day, so we multiply (XL + IL) by 24 and then by the night set-back factor, .95. Then we multiply the product by DD/65 or SDD/65 to get the daily or seasonal heat loss. You now have most of the basic ideas you need to be your own heating engineer and to compute the heat losses of your home, now, and as you improve it.

YOUR FUEL BILL IN MBTU

You will be interested in converting the heat loss of your home into dollars or dollars into heat loss. First you must know the conversion heat content of your fuel and the price of your fuel.

In this book we shall assume oil as our heat source. The conversion heat content of a fuel is obtained by multiplying the heat content of the fuel by the conversion efficiency of the burner. For oil, the conversion heat content is about 100,000 Btu per gallon. We shall assume a price of 50¢ a gallon now and an increase to $1.20 per gallon in 10 years. At this heat content and 50¢ per gallon, fuel oil costs $5 per MBTU.

The conversion heat content of natural gas is about 700 Btu per cubic feet. If you pay for your gas in cubic feet, you can readily exchange dollars and Btu by this conversion factor. Some natural gas people like to think of their product in therms, which is 100,000 Btu. If you buy your gas in therms, you have to multiply the number of therms you use by 65%, the conversion efficiency of your gas burner, to get the Btu output of your furnace. Gas at 30¢ per therm is $4.60 per MBTU.

If you use electric resistance heat, one kilowatt-hour is the heat equivalent of 3413 Btu. Your electric resistance heat has an efficiency of 100%, but, at the generating station, the conversion efficiency is only about 40%. You therefore pay more per Btu for electric heat than for other sources. You can easily determine your heating load in Btu by multiplying the KWHR on your electric bill by 3413. Electricity at 5¢ per KWHR is $14.65 per MBTU.

If you get your fuel oil delivered from a dealer on a contract basis, he can probably tell you what your yearly consumption is. If you get it on a delivery basis, you will have to try to figure it out the way you figure your miles per gallon of driving a car. If you mix services other than space heating with gas or electricity, you will have to estimate the portion due to space heating by deducting the amount you use in a period when you do not use space conditioning. You really should make an effort to determine your actual usage in Btu because we are going to ask you to take a theoretical survey of your home's heating needs in terms of Btu load. The only way you can know whether you are taking a good survey is to compare your theoretical results with your actual consumption. For example, if calculations show that your heating load was 140 MBTU, with 50¢ oil your fuel bill should be $700. Conversely, if your fuel bill were $700, your heating load should calculate out to about 140 MBTU.

THE FM HOME

One of the handiest devices for the kind of thing we are doing is to have a model against which samples can be measured. We need a figure of merit house—let us call it the FM home.

First, let us assume that the FM home has 1000 square feet of conditioned floor space. That number makes it easy to compare your own home with the FM home. If your home has 1400 square feet of floor, you need only multiply the total heat loss of the FM home by 1.4 and compare the answer with your own total heat loss to see how you rate.

Let the FM home have an aspect ratio of 25 × 40 feet. The floor is over a four-foot basement. The basement has concrete walls and a concrete floor. We specify this type of design so that we can discount heat transfer through the floors in our initial considerations. It has 100 square feet of window distributed as 30 north, 15 east, 40 south and 15 west. The sash length allowance is 1.3 times the square footage, or 130 linear feet. There are two doors for 38 square feet of surface exposure. The perimeter of the house is 130 feet, and the wall height is 9 feet, giving a gross wall exposure of 170 square feet. Subtracting the window and door area, we have a net wall area of 1034 square feet. The ceiling area is 1000 square feet. Gable ends are not counted because they are a part of the attic space. There is a basement furnace but no fireplace.

THE AU GROUPS

The minute we try to set up a model or typical home we find that it cannot be done. There are too many variables. Homes vary from no insulation to heavy insulation, windows vary from loose, single pane types to new triple pane types, climates vary from under 500 DD to over 10,000 DD. There does not seem to be much promise that we can work out an FM home.

Before we give up the FM home idea let us take another tack. Our proposed FM home is of the 1000 square foot category, and it has 100 square feet of window. That is, the window area is 10% of the floor area. We will find that most homes have window areas of around 10% of the floor area. If your homes does not have 10% window area you can compare it with one having 10% area by a simple ratio procedure. Wall area will also have a fairly uniform relation to floor area. Therefore, we may be able to find some commonality by looking at the product of U, the factor with the most variation, and area, the factor with some uniformity.

Let us explore in Table 2-1 how the different construction features affect the AU factor of the heat loss equations. A frame wall may typically have no insulation, a layer of R7 (2″), a layer of R11 (4″), a layer of R19 (6″), or R19 with insulating board on the outside. Table 2-1 shows the AU value for the composite walls for each of these variations. We find that we can also categorize ceilings, windows and doors by increasing degrees of heat conservation.

THE FM CLASSES

We can now discover a very interesting interpretation of Table 2-1. The AU factors can be put together in significant sets characterized by their increasing attention to conservation measures. If there is a home with no insulation in the walls and single pane windows, it probably has no insulation in the attic and no storm doors, and it probably has a high infiltration rate. It is a very drafty home.

TABLE 2-1. AU FACTORS FOR FRAME BUILDINGS

CEILING	AU	WALLS	AU
No Insulation	590	No Insulation	253
R7	115	R7	233
R11	79	R11	99
R19	48	R19	71
R30	32	R30	30

WINDOWS	AU	DOORS	AU
Single	115	No storm	7.99–8.09
Double	40–60	With storm	2.5–5.27
Triple	36		

	INFILTRATION FACTORS		
	WALLS–VU	WINDOWS–VU	DOORS–VU
Grade 1	557.0	468.0	68.3
Grade 2	93.0	211.0	34.2
Grade 3	18.3	211.0	25.6
Grade 4	9.3	70.0	17.1
Grade 5	1.9	21.6	5.3

NOTE: In figuring the Btu's required to heat air we use volume of air instead of area of surface. The transmission coefficient is a constant instead of a variable, as it is with other materials. The air coefficient has the same function as U in the heat loss equations, so for our convenience here we call it "U." For the infiltration of cold air into the home we call the category factor "VU" instead of "AU."

Then there might be the average home with still no wall insulation and single pane windows but with token insulation in the attic and an effort to caulk and weatherstrip the doors and windows.

Next we can identify a class built by developers in recent years to meet federal minimum property standards because only such houses could get government insured loans. We might call this set the Modern class.

Now we see coming upon the scene something new in specifications, the ASHRAE standard 90–75, "Energy Conservation in New Building Design." This standard was developed by ASHRAE (American Society of Heating, Refrigerating and Air-Conditioning Engineers) as a means of promulgating what heating engineers consider to be reasonable and attainable methods of reducing the energy budget of new buildings. This standard has been adopted by some states and localities as a part of the building code. We might identify this set as the 90–75 class.

The people who wrote 90–75 said, "Look, fellows, we don't mean that you have to stop here. Our specification is just the very least you can do to conserve energy." People who want to do better than 90–75 can do better. We might rate the homes these people build as the Superior class.

People who really are committed to the new age of conservation can do even better than build to the Superior class standards. We might call this set the Ultra class.

We have now identified six classes of homes based on the quality of their energy conservation. In Table 2-1 the AU factors fall into six typical characteristics for walls, attics, windows and doors. We can rearrange these groups into sets as shown in Table 2-2. These sets now become exhibited as the Drafty class, the Average class, the Modern class, the 90–75 class, the Superior class and the Ultra class.

TABLE 2-2. FM HOMES IDENTIFIED BY CLASS OF AU FACTORS

SECTION	DRAFTY	AVERAGE	MODERN	SUPERIOR	ULTRA
Attic	590	115	79	32	25
Windows	115	115	60	40	36
Walls	253	233	99	71	30
Doors	8	8	5	2.5	2.5
Infiltration	1093	372	263	96	29
TOTAL	2059	843	506	242	122

NOTE: Specifications for the 90–75 class do not lend themselves to the AU class interpretation.

With the AU factors arranged in sets as seen in Table 2-2 we are able to recognize six distinct classes of homes characterized by their attention to heat conservation. We have six energy classes of homes built to the FM home dimensions. We can say, then, that we have categorized six typical homes, or, we can say that we have identified six classes of FM homes.

This discovery is significant because we can locate our own home on a sliding scale of energy efficiency. We can set our goal to something tangible. If, after we take a survey of our home, we find that it is in the Average class, we can aim to upgrade it to the Modern class or even to the Superior class. By comparing our own AU factors for walls, attic, windows and doors we can pinpoint where some of our trouble lies. We can

Most American homes lose heat about according to this diagram.

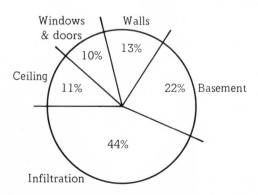

set up an intelligent, long-term program of upgrading. We can tune our home improvements and modernization to these energy efficient goals.

Some of the following chapters show you how to determine the AU factors and heat losses for the various sections of your home.

MASONRY FM HOMES

Table 2-2 identifies FM classes of homes having frame construction. What about homes with masonry walls?

Masonry walls come in a much bigger variety of construction types than frame walls. We see face brick with interior frame and gypsum board, two layers of brick with interior gypsum board, stucco and concrete block or poured concrete with interior gypsum board. Some masonry walls do not have an interior facing of gypsum or other finish. Some masonry walls are solid, and some have a cavity wall between layers. Some bricks are solid, and some have air cells. Masonry materials vary widely in density, and density influences U value. There are three main ways to insulate masonry: Perlite or Vermiculite may be poured into the cells of bricks or blocks; polyurethane or polystyrene board or bat insulation or foam may be placed in the cavity wall; bat or roll insulation or insulating board or foam may be placed between the gypsum board and the wall. And then there is the bright new idea of putting the insulation on the outside of the masonry wall.

Unless you were there when it was built or have some documentary proof of construction, you probably will have only the haziest of ideas as to what type of masonry wall you have.

In spite of these variations in construction, there is not too great a variation in U values. For uninsulated brick or block walls the range of U is from .26 to .37, with an average of .32. For uninsulated poured concrete the U range is from .21 to .28, with an average of .25. Thus, for an uninsulated masonry wall the U average is from .02 to .08 higher than for uninsulated frame walls. However, masonry has what is called "capacity insulation." It takes longer for heat to pass through a masonry wall than a frame wall. This slower reaction time acts like a U value, or, effectively, serves to reduce the nominal U value of masonry. By slowing down the reaction time, masonry acts like insulation; hence, we can see why it is called capacity insulation. This thermal lag causes uninsulated frame and uninsulated masonry to lose about the same amount of heat over a thermal cycle. Therefore, we put uninsulated frame and uninsulated masonry walls in the same AU group.

We find that the insulated masonry wall U value ranges from .06 to .08, with an average at .073. Since this U value is about that of the R11 frame wall, we put insulated masonry in the R11 group of frame walls.

These considerations put uninsulated masonry homes in the FM Drafty class and the insulated masonry homes in the FM Modern class.

IDENTIFYING YOUR HOME

You can tell where your own home is on the energy efficiency scale by combining Table 2-2 with your cost of fuel and your local annual degree days.

First, convert your fuel dollars into MBTU, using the conversion factors we described earlier. For example, if we use fuel oil and pay 50¢ a gallon, we pay 50¢ per 100,000 Btu. Simply moving the decimal place one digit to the right gives us $5 per 1,000,000 Btu. That is we pay $5 per MBTU. Assume our fuel bill was $900. Then, 900/5 = 180 MBTU. If we paid 43¢ a gallon for fuel, our cost per MBTU is $4.30, and our energy cost is 900/4.3 = 209.3 MBTU.

Next, work out the ratio between the floor area of your own home and the 1000 square footage of the FM home. For example, if your home has 1200 square feet of floor space, it is 1.2 times larger than the FM home, and the fuel expenditure should be 1.2 larger.

Now work out the adjusted seasonal heat loss for the several classes of FM homes using this equation:

$$S = (AU) \times Td \times 24 \times .95 \times DD/65 \times R$$

where (AU) = all the AU factor totals in Table 2-2
are R = the area ratio between your own home and the FM home.

After you have made these calculations, compare your own heat loss. What class fits your home?

For example, assume 180 MBTU fuel consumption, 6000 DD climate and Td of 70. The Average class home works out to 144 MBTU, which is 36 MBTU lower than your own consumption. There are several reasons for the discrepancy, such as, your home may have a very different configuration from the FM home. Table 2-2 does not take into account the basement losses. (We have deliberately left out basement losses because there are too many variations.) Basement losses can account for 20% of the heating load of a home. Since 20% of 180 MBTU is 36 MBTU, we judge our home to be in the Average class.

Other books to read about conservation and solar energy are: *Direct Use of the Sun's Energy,* Farrington Daniels; *The Solar Home Book,* Bruce Anderson, from Total Environmental Action, Harrisville, NH; *Design Criteria for Solar-Heated Buildings,* Barber and Watson, from Sunworks, Inc., Guilford, CT 06437; *Making the Most of Your Energy Dollars,* Bureau of Standards publication #C13.53.8, from Superintendent of Documents, Government Printing Office, Washington, DC 20402; *ASHRAE Standard 90–75,* "Energy Conservation in New Building Design," from ASHRAE Headquarters, 345 E. 47th St., New York, NY 10017; *Solar Control and Shading Devices,* from Princeton University Press, Princeton, NJ; *Minimum Design Standards for Heat Loss Calculations,* U.S. Department of Housing and Urban Development, Washington, DC 20410; *Solar Energy Thermal Process,* John A. Duffy and William Beckman (very technical); *Solar Energy Utilization for Heating and Cooling,* John I. Yellott (technical); and *Solar Dwelling Design Concepts,* from American Institute of Architects Research Corporation.

Another source of solar energy books is SUNWAY, 1301 Berkeley Way, Berkeley, CA 94702.

3

What To Do About Attics

PROCEDURES

Our basic proposition in this book is that you should first determine where you are, then plan where you want to go and then carry out the steps necessary to get there. We assume that you have already decided which of the classes of FM home your own home matches. Now your problem is to determine where the attic of your home stands.

First you need to do a hands-on inspection of the attic. We trust that you are able to climb into it, or at least look into it. You may find nothing there except the ceiling attached to the joists, there may be some insulation and there may be flooring laid above the joists. If there is insulation, note what kind it is and how thick it is. If it is bat or roll insulation, it should tell you on the side next to the ceiling what the thickness is. If there is flooring make sure whether there is insulation below and, if so, how thick it is. Note the amount and kind of attic ventilation, if any.

Next, determine the area of your attic. Do not assume that the attic area is a simple function of the perimeter of the house. You should actually measure it. There may be vertical sections as well as horizontal sections. If the vertical sections are walls to heated spaces, they should be insulated.

If the attic is open to an area over an unheated room, this area should also be insulated. It will be difficult for you to estimate how much heat loss you pay through this ceiling without insulation, but you may be sure it is considerable.

If some of the ceiling is attached to the same rafters as the roof, as will be the case in cathedral ceilings or rooms built into gables or dormer rooms, you must consider these areas as part of the attic. You may have to compute the heat loss for these areas separately.

The R values of the materials you will probably find in the attic are found in the following list:

Gypsum board	.32
Lath & plaster	.10
Pine flooring	.94

Roof sheathing	1.32
Wood shingles	.99
Asphalt shingles	.44
Inside air	.68
Outside air	.17
2″ insulation	7
3 1/2″ insulation	11
6″ insulation	19

To compute the U value of your attic ceiling, add the R values of the materials involved from the above list and take the reciprocal. For example:

Inside air	.68	
Gypsum board	.32	
Inside air	.68	
R total	1.68	U, 1/1.68 = .6
Add R11	11	
New total	12.68	U, 1/12.68 = .08

To compute the heat loss equation you must have the temperature difference, Td, between the design temperature and the thermostat setting. You get the design temperature close enough for your own purposes by knowing how cold it is likely to get on a very cold night. The design temperature is the reading on the outdoor thermometer.

You have a different problem when it comes to attics. Your Td must be the difference between the thermostat setting and the attic temperature, and that temperature is not likely to be the same as the outdoor temperature. During the day heat will accumulate in the attic from heat loss from the house and from solar heat on the roof. During the night heat will accumulate from heat loss from the house.

There are complex equations enabling you to figure out what your attic temperature is likely to be. We have summarized the results of these equations for a number of different situations in Table 3-1. In column one we list a range of design temperatures. In the rest of the columns we list the computed temperatures of the attic for different grades of insulation for the design temperatures. To obtain Td find the appropriate number in the table and subtract it from the thermostat setting. For example, the

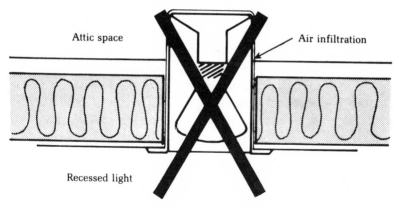

Avoid Recessed Lights and
Leakage Through the Ceiling Fixtures

design temperature is 0, the thermostat is 70, and, from the table, the attic temperature is 11. Td is therefore 59.

TABLE 3-1.   ATTIC TEMPERATURES

Design Temp.	No Insul.	R7	R11	R19	R30	R38
40	58	48	47	45	44	44
30	53	40	37	36	34	34
20	49	31	28	26	24	23
10	44	22	19	16	15	14
0	40	15	11	8	6	5
−10	35	5	1	−3	−5	−7
−20	30	−3	−8	−12	−15	−16

You must treat those cathedral ceilings or dormer ceilings as composite sections. That is, you must add the R values of the ceiling and the roof and take the reciprocal to find the U value. For example,

Inside air below ceiling	.68
Gypsum board	.32
Inside air above ceiling	.68
Roof sheathing	1.32
Asphalt shingles	.44
Outside air	.17
R total	3.61 U, 1/3.61 = .28

Td for these ceilings will be the regular outdoor design temperature. However, these ceilings present a special problem if they face east, south or west because there will be a considerable amount of heat gain into the space between rafters on sunny days. Our suggestion is that you add 10 degrees to the design temperature for south roofs and 5 degrees for east or west roofs before computing the Td value. Cathedral ceilings are aesthetically pleasing in many homes. One can only wonder whether they will be used very much in the future, considering their energy problems.

THE FM ATTIC

In Table 3-2 we list the computed heat loss for the various FM classes. This table illustrates the characteristic amounts of improvement you obtain as you increase the amount of attic insulation.

We recommend that you figure out the class of energy efficiency characteristic of your home and then set your aim to attain one, two or three grades above. If your home is of the Average class, you should aim for the Modern, Superior or Ultra class. We do not necessarily recommend that you consult Table 3-2 and then at once install, say, R19 insulation. Rather, you should make attic upgrading a part of your total scheme of upgrading. Perhaps you will discover that windows are giving you a more serious problem than your attic. In other words, attack the whole problem and deal with worst things first. Do not be stampeded into attic insulation just because everyone from the government to the salesmen is trying to talk you into it.

TABLE 3-2. ATTIC HEAT LOSS OF FM HOMES, MBTU

AU		590	115	79	48	32	25
Td	DD	DRAFTY	AVERAGE	MODERN	90–75	SUPERIOR	ULTRA
34	1000	7.04	1.37	.94	.57	.38	.298
47	2000	19.45	3.79	2.60	1.58	1.05	.824
54	3000	33.50	6.53	4.49	2.73	1.82	1.420
58	4000	48.00	9.35	6.43	3.90	2.60	2.030
63	5000	65.19	12.70	8.73	5.30	3.50	2.760
70	6000	86.92	16.96	11.64	7.07	4.71	3.680
77	7000	111.50	21.70	14.93	9.08	6.05	4.730
82	8000	135.75	26.46	18.18	11.04	7.36	5.750
86	9000	160.20	31.22	21.45	13.03	8.69	6.790
92	10,000	190.40	37.11	25.49	15.49	10.33	8.070

ADDING ATTIC INSULATION

When you get down to the nitty-gritty details of adding attic insulation, there are certain practical considerations.

There is, of course, the decision to be made whether to do it yourself or hire it done. If there is easy access to the attic and you are handy, you can easily do it yourself and save about 50%.

Vendors will probably talk to you about putting in 6 inches of insulation because its R19 value is what conservation-minded bureaucrats want. R19 may not be what you want, however. If you do your calculations well, you will know what you want and should insist on it.

There are two main types of insulation available for retrofit of attics: bat or roll type, and loose type. The bat or roll type is simply laid down between the joists. The loose type can be poured from a bag or blown in by machine. If you do it yourself, you will have to pour in loose insulation by hand, although there are a few vendors around who rent the machines for blowing insulation. Foam insulation is not generally recommended for attics, although this situation may change with some new products. You should be alert to the possibility of new and better insulation that may come along. With all of the drive to get every home insulated, inventive genius will be sure to come up with many new ideas.

Classified by material, you have three main choices: fiberglass, mineral wool and cellulose or converted paper. It is not our purpose here to appraise the value of one over the other. Each is capable of performing a good job, or it would not continue to be sold. Often your choice will be based on price, convenience, availability or vendor qualifications.

Fiberglass and mineral wool are fireproof. Mineral wool is slightly heavier than fiberglass and may tend to press down insulation already there. If the vendor guarantees cellulose to be Class I insulation, it is fire resistant to 1200 degrees.

Some of the criteria for judging insulation are:

- What is its R value? Who has tested and certified the R value?
- Will it retain its R value for at least 20 years?
- Is it vermin-proof?
- Is it fire resistant?
- In case of fire, will it give off noxious fumes?
- If you already have insulation, what will happen to it if insulation is put on top? Will it be compressed and lose some of its R value?

The cost of attic insulation will run about 40¢ to 50¢ a square foot from professional installers, or half that if you do it yourself. (1978 dollars.)

You can get an idea of the payback period for attic insulation by referring to Table 3-2. Assume that you have a Drafty home, without attic insulation, in a 6000 DD climate and that you can buy R7 insulation for 30¢ a square foot. If you were to upgrade the Drafty home to an Average home by adding R7 to the attic, you would save 70 MBTU, or $350, per year. You would pay for the insulation in less than a year. Assume that you have a Modern home in a 6000 DD climate and wish to upgrade to the Superior class by adding R19 to your R11 insulation. Assume you could buy R19 for 50¢ a square foot. You would save about 7 MBTU, or $35, a year, and it would take more than 14 years to pay back the $500 cost.

Careful investigation of this sort will tell you whether it is wise to insulate your attic or go after some other saving. We do not want you to hesitate to move your attic from the Modern to the Superior class just because it will take 14 years to pay for the upgrading. Our predictions are that fossil energy will more than double in 14 years, so the payback period will actually be less. What we do say is that as you look more and more into conservation and into the virtues of self-sufficient energy you will come to have a slightly different motive for upgrading and will seek to move to the Superior or Ultra class so as to obtain a lot of benefits in addition to money saving, or payback.

SPECIAL PROBLEMS

Do your eaves project about a foot or so beyond the sidewall? If so, note whether there are louvers in the fascia boards. Louvers mean that the designer has included eave ventilation as a part of attic ventilation. In this case there is supposed to be ventilation from the eave louvers to the louvers in the gable ends. Added insulation must not block this air passage. Blown insulation may have a special difficulty near eave vents; the air movement may gradually blow the insulation away from the air path, reducing the thickness, and the R value, of the insulation in this area. This situation can be avoided by placing a strip of bat type insulation about 3 feet long near the vent, instead of loose or blown insulation. If you do not have eave louvers, make sure that the insulation fits snugly up against the rafter plate.

You can find differing opinions on whether attic insulation needs a vapor barrier. Water, of course, is worthless as insulation. If water vapor from inside the house gets through the walls and into the insulation, the outside cold will cause the vapor to condense into water. The insulation becomes wet and loses its ability to resist the passage of heat. Attics offer a little different situation from walls. Those who would skip attic vapor barriers argue that good attic ventilation prevents the condensation of moisture. We are inclined to favor the argument that vapor barriers should be included wherever possible. For example, ceilings over high moisture areas such as kitchens and bathrooms are almost sure to show beam shadows over the years if they are lacking a vapor barrier.

The vapor barrier problem is one argument against blown insulation for retrofit of attics. Bat or roll type insulation almost always has a strip of vapor barrier, which is installed facing the interior of the building. If your attic already has a layer of bat or roll insulation with a vapor barrier, then a layer of blown insulation on top of it is good. If your installer will put in vapor barrier in an uninsulated attic, at least over the bath and kitchen, then blown insulation is good.

Roll or bat type insulation with a vapor barrier should not be laid over insulation already in place. If insulation with the vapor barrier must be used because the plain type is not available, then the installer must slash large cuts in barrier sheet.

There is one situation you must watch out for when buying blown insulation from a vendor who installs it. The resistance value of blown insulation depends on both the thickness and on the density or weight of the material per square foot. Furthermore, density varies with manufacturers. The density depends on the number of square feet covered by a bag of material. When dealing with a blown insulation vendor you should require him to state in his contract the number of square feet per bag his insulation will cover for the required R value. All manufacturers supplying to Federal Specification HH–1–1030 are required to put this information on the label. You can check the label when he comes to do his work to make sure he is living up to his contract.

We have already referred to some of the problems encountered with cathedral, dormer and gable ceilings. We are not through yet. They are almost an insoluble problem if you want to upgrade their insulation. It is considered a serious mistake to fill the entire rafter space between ceiling and roof with insulation. Some amount of air space is essential. If there is no air circulation in this space, the heat build-up during the day followed by the rapid cooling at night will cause the roofing to buckle and crack. A 20-year roof can go to pieces in a few years with this situation. With no air circulation there can be severe moisture problems, particularly with wood shingles. With 6 inch rafters your only solution is 2 inch roll type insulation with a vapor barrier next to the ceiling. If you already have this insulation in place, do not let any vendor sell you on the idea of adding more. Blown or poured insulation should not be used in this space partly because of the difficulty of controlling the depth and partly because there is a tendency for it to slide to the lower end and fill it up, if there is any slope.

One of the most serious of the special problems has nothing to do with insulation but with the credibility of the vendors. Unfortunately, many insulation vendors are salesmen only; they are not heating engineers. They are prepared to tell you the advantages, real or imagined, of their product and to reveal the faults of the competitor product, but hard technical questions will floor many of them. Many of their statements are in conflict with statements made by other vendors. Whom shall we believe? One helpful guide is to ask the salesman to figure out the heat loss of your attic. A great many of them cannot do it. Many of them will try to beg off by saying, "Oh, you'll save 50% on your fuel bill." But, as we saw above, such a statement is not necessarily true. If the salesman cannot figure out your heat loss, it means that you must depend on yourself to do the figuring. The product may be satisfactory even when the salesman isn't. Another guide is to inquire about the length of time the vendor has been in business and to ask for names of customers so that you can check up on the vendor's dependability.

Even if you decide that you have enough insulation, it will be wise to inspect the quality of workmanship in the installation that you already have. Time was when insulation was laid down in a careless manner because it was not considered that important. Make sure that it fits snugly at the eaves and around chimneys. Check the electrical entrances of ceiling lights. You may find two errors there. The knockouts and other gaps in electrical boxes can offer an active route for air infiltration. Make sure these gaps are stuffed with insulation such as fiberglass or mineral wool. The other error may be in the way the insulation is laid over the electrical wire. Unless the roll type insulation is torn apart a little and tucked in and around the wire, there may be a gaping hole, which is both a straight line for air infiltration and a loss of R value at this point.

ATTIC VENTILATION

While you are doing something about attic insulation you might as well check out the attic ventilation. Some will maintain that attic vents should be closed in winter and open in summer. Open vents in winter are needed

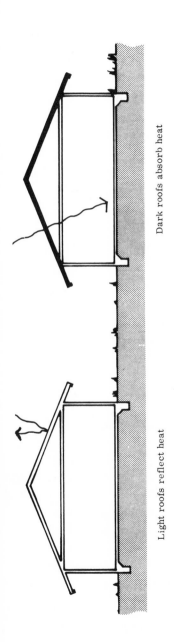

Light roofs reflect heat

Dark roofs absorb heat

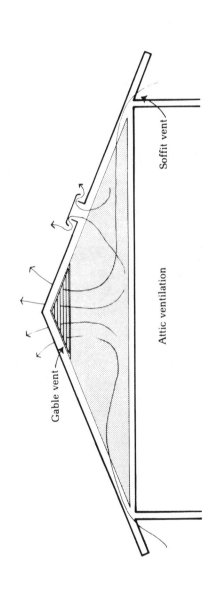

Gable vent

Soffit vent

Attic ventilation

in climates that have alternating periods of mild, moist weather followed by cold, dry air. Moist air gets into the attic by infiltration and then condenses when the weather turns colder. With open vents the moist air is cleared out by the incoming dry air before the vapor has time to condense.

Cross ventilation with gable vents at either end and gable vents on L-projections should be provided. According to FHA Minimum Property Standards, gable vents for attics without vapor barrier should provide 1 square foot opening for each 150 square feet of ceiling. For attics with a vapor barrier, the least vent area should be 1 square foot for each 300 square foot of opening for each 150 square feet of ceiling. For attics with a vapor barrier, the least vent area should be 1 square foot for each 300 the net vent area. With rain louvers and 1/4" hardware cloth, the gross area should be double the specified net area. Mesh openings of 1/8" require gross openings of 2 1/2 times the net area, and mesh openings of 1/16" require gross openings 3 times the net area specification.

In southern climates forced attic ventilation is desirable. It is especially desirable if the attic insulation is below R19. In mid-climates where there are less than 600 summer cooling hours the cost of operating a fan is more than the savings that result from less frequent operation of an air conditioner.

When fans are chosen, the capacity should be about 1 1/2 times the area of the ceiling. For example, a 1000 square foot ceiling should require a fan capable of delivering air at the rate of 1500 cubic feet per minute. The fan should be thermostatically controlled to operate automatically.

With the rising emphasis on conservation, you will find attic fans being pushed vigorously by the salesmen. Before responding to the sales pitch you should evaluate carefully to determine whether it is economically advantageous to install an attic fan. We estimate that a house with 1000 square feet of attic and R7 insulation will have a heat gain of about 7 MBTU through the ceiling during a 1000 hour cooling season. We estimate that an attic fan could reduce this heat gain to about 4 MBTU. However, if we were to add R11 on top of the R7 the heat gain would be reduced to about 2.5 MBTU. Assuming about $50 for the cost of the fan and about $50 installation charges, the prorated original cost and the operating costs (it costs money to run the fan) will amount to about $20 per season. The cost of R19 would be about $6 for the cooling season. Since we want at least R19 in most climates to reduce the winter heat loss, there is clearly no great benefit, usually, to be derived from an attic fan. We encourage you to be guided by the rational. Don't spend energy to save energy if you can save it easier and cheaper by passive means.

In those climates with over 1000 hours of cooling season and summer design temperatures in the high 90's, analysis may very well show that, even with heavy insulation, an attic fan will cut down on air conditioner hours. Since the fan is cheaper to operate than the air conditioner, it would make sense to spend energy to save energy in this case.

REPLACEMENT OF CEILINGS

Do you have an unsightly ceiling that has disturbed you for some time? Now you can use the energy crunch as the reason to do something about it.

The usual way to fix a bad ceiling is to cover it with ceiling tile. Metal hangers are attached to the ceiling and the tile slid into the hangers. Now is the time to put an inch or two of insulating board on the ceiling before the hangers are attached.

Insulating board has an R value of 3 to 4 depending on the type chosen. Ceiling tile itself has an R value of 1.23. Thus, you can easily add at least R4.23 to the attic insulation above those rooms so upgraded.

If your home has 10-foot ceilings you may wish to bring the height down to a more normal level, say 8 feet. On a typical winter day lower ceilings would save you about 200 Btuh. The ceiling tile method is again the usual approach. In this case the tile carriers are suspended from the

ceiling by metal hangers. Do not miss this opportunity to add insulation. There are two ways to do it. In one case you may attach insulating board to the ceiling before attaching the hangers. In the other case you may add extra hangers to carry the additional weight and then lay bat type insulation across the carriers before inserting the tile.

In later chapters we will discuss the need for distributing the extra heat of one room to other parts of the house. This idea requires a place to put the ducts. The space above a suspended ceiling is the ideal place. If you want to lower your ceilings, think about this angle before going ahead.

If you already have suspended ceilings you may wonder about the practicality of adding blown insulation above the tile. Often it may be difficult or impossible to add insulation above the original ceiling. While blown insulation is light, the suspension system and ceiling tile are not intended to carry the extra weight. The best way to add insulation in this case is to remove the tile, which is easy, and then proceed much as you would from the beginning. Attach insulating board to the original ceiling, or add extra hangers and lay in the bat type insulation.

4

What To Do
About Windows

There are three factors—heat gain, heat loss by infiltration, and heat loss by conduction—that affect the performance of a window in your home. We need to think about each of them before deciding how to upgrade our windows.

CONVERSION OF LIGHT TO HEAT

The glass people have been very successful in selling their product to architects and home builders. Now we are saying that glass lets in too much cold or too much heat. When it admits too much heat, we are told to use a heat absorbing glass or a heat absorbing film. We should become a little more sophisticated.

Solar energy technology has taught us the importance of knowing more about the solar spectrum and about how solar radiation gets converted to heat. The most intense part of the solar radiation reaching us is in the visible and near-infrared spectrum. When this band of solar energy strikes the glass of a home, about 15% of it gets reflected away, and the rest enters the room and becomes available for conversion to heat.

Here is what happens: Solar radiation enters the room and is absorbed by the things in the room, such as the floor, the rug, the furniture and the walls. Some things absorb more radiation than others. If a material is black or a dark color, it means that the material is absorbing almost all of the radiation. When a material absorbs radiation, it means that the light rays are making the little atoms dance and kick around, and, when atoms get that excited they feel warm to the touch. The things in a room exhibit a higher temperature, either to our bodies or to a thermometer. We say that the things in the room have acquired sensible heat. The radiated energy has converted the atoms of things to a higher energy state, which we sense as heat.

HEAT GAIN

This increase in the sensible heat of the things in a room constitutes the amount of heat gain induced by the solar radiation through the windows. One important idea to keep in mind is that windows permit heat gain only during daylight. At night glass acts as pure transmission heat loss. To obtain maximum heat gain, the glass surface and the absorbing material must face the sun's rays squarely—be "normal" to the sun, as this angle is called. Since this condition prevails only rarely, the heat gain in a room is almost always less than maximum. In computing the heat gain into the room, we prefer to lean on the concepts of solar engineering.

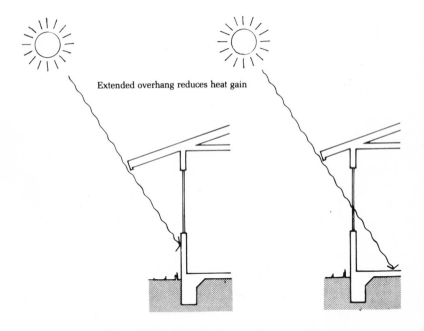

Extended overhang reduces heat gain

Solar engineers, attempting to collect maximum solar energy, have a problem with a fixed collector because the sun's angle changes in both azimuth and elevation from moment to moment and day to day. They could rotate the collector to follow the sun, but that solution is expensive, and they generally avoid it. They usually set the collector at some optimum angle and take the consequences. Windows, when they act as solar collectors, are at an even greater disadvantage. They are never at optimum angle. However, it is interesting to note that, at most latitudes, south windows have greater heat gain in winter than in summer because, as the sun dips further south in winter, it is more nearly normal to the glass. We note the surprising fact that in March the amount of insolation (the solar engineer's term for the rate of delivery of solar radiation) on a south window in Maine is 1 1/2 times greater than in south Florida. In January the insolation on a vertical south window is about the same all over the country, except in the extreme north.

The amount of solar radiation passing through a window is greatest on a clear, bright day. This condition prevails only part of the time because of the clouds. To have an average figure to work with, we take 60% as the probable amount of cloudless daylight. This figure is optimistic because in some regions the per cent of cloudless sky in winter is 50% or less.

Daylight has two components, direct and diffuse. Direct sunlight is what shines in a direct line from the sun. As the direct rays come through the atmosphere some of them are scattered by the air molecules and the dust and the water vapor. These light rays bounce around in all directions as they get reflected from one particle to another. The whole dome of the sky is bright because of this diffuse radiation. If it was not for the diffuse light, the sun would be a bright spot in a black sky. This diffuse light can be converted to heat just the same as can direct sunlight. The difference is that the intensity of diffuse light is much less and therefore the amount converted is less.

In Table 4-1 we derive the approximate amount of heat gain you can expect from a south window for each square foot of glass. The decimal numbers in the columns refer to millions of Btu. We derive the numbers for 5 latitudes between 24 degrees and 56 degrees. If you live between these latitudes, you can interpolate to your own latitude with sufficient accuracy.

We adapt the *insolation* column from Table 1, page 387, ASHRAE's 1972 "Handbook of Fundamentals." We derive the *clearness* column by multiplying the insolation column by .60 to account for the fact that clouds probably obscure the sun at least 40% of the time.

TABLE 4-1. HEAT GAIN, MBTU PER SQUARE FOOT OF A VERTICAL SOUTH WINDOW FOR THE HEATING SEASON

	SOLAR IRRADIATION			
Latitude	Insolation	Clearness	Diffuse	Total
24	.298	.179	.036	.215
32	.322	.193	.038	.231
40	.323	.194	.040	.234
48	.310	.186	.038	.224
56	.260	.156	.032	.188

TABLE 4-1 (continued)

	SOLAR COLLECTION		
Latitude	Single Glass	Efficiency	Double Glass
24	.111	.095	.081
32	.119	.102	.087
40	.120	.103	.089
48	.116	.099	.085
56	.097	.083	.075

To determine the amount of diffuse radiation available for conversion we have followed a method developed by Coleman of Total Environmental Action, Harrisville, New Hampshire (Jeremy J. Coleman, "Estimating Average Long-Term Daily Radiation Striking Tilted Surfaces," Proceedings of NESEA Conference, 1976). We list these computed values in the *diffuse* column.

We derive the total insolation by adding the *clearness* column and the *diffuse* column.

The *total* column is the amount of energy available for conversion as it arrives at the outside of the glass of a south window. Solar radiation has to get through the glass before it can be converted to heat in your home. Some of this energy is lost because the glass reflects and absorbs some of it. The DS (double strength) sheet glass you probably have in your windows is generally assumed to transmit about 86% of the irradiation reaching it. We must multiply the *total* column by .86 to obtain the amount of energy actually available for conversion inside your home. We list these amounts in the *single glass* column, which refers to the fact that we are first considering only the case of the single pane window.

We have noted that visible light gets converted to heat once it has passed into the room. Unfortunately, there is not very much information to guide us in estimating how much of this energy gets converted to heat. A good, black absorbing surface will convert more than 95% of the solar radiation into heat. Almost no object in a normal home qualifies as a good absorber. We are going to assume 60% as the conversion efficiency of a room, although that percentage is optimistic because good flat plate collectors can seldom do better. We multiply the *single glass* column by .60 and list the results in the *efficiency* column.

We now have what you have been looking for—the amount of heat in MBTU you can reasonably expect to get per square foot of south window during a heating season from October through April. The decimal numbers in the *efficiency* column give you that information. These numbers are, of course, approximations.

In some cases it will be necessary to determine the heat gain from windows with double pane glass. In this case you must include another .86 derating factor. In the *double glass* column we have multiplied the *efficiency* column by .86 to obtain the seasonal heat gain for this situation.

To determine the heat gain for windows having access to sunlight but not facing south, use a derating factor. We recommend reducing the south window value to .75 for southeast or southwest windows and to .60 for east or west windows.

North windows are notorious villains for the heating engineer. They do not admit direct sunlight, and they seem to pour heat out of the house at a great rate. Let us see. Remember that diffuse light covers the entire sky dome. It is uniformly distributed, and just as much of it strikes the north window as the south. Since diffuse light can be converted to heat, the north windows must therefore be capable of contributing some heat.

Let us compute as an example the diffuse gain at 40 degrees latitude in a 5000 DD climate. We find that the heat loss from a square foot of north window is .141 MBTU for the season and the gain is .02 MBTU (.04 × .86 × .6). The heat loss can be discounted by 14% due to the heat gain. If the north window were upgraded to one-fourth that heat loss, the heat gain would be 57% of the heat loss.

INFILTRATION LOSSES

We say in Chapter 2 that the annual heat loss from infiltration can be calculated with the equation

$$IL = V \times .018 \times 24 \times DD/65$$

The trick is to find the volume, V, of air that enters a window by infiltration. Even engineers who design new buildings and have laboratory data to work with have to temper their calculations with judgment. The best you can hope for with an old window is to come up with an educated guess.

To help you educate your guesses, we have taken ASHRAE data and other sources and have compiled approximations in Table 4-2. We are suggesting the "crack method" as the best way to estimate infiltration for an established house. Some methods assume one to two air changes per hour, but that method does not seem to be reliable enough for our purposes. The crack method requires that you estimate the air volume leakage per linear foot per hour and multiply that estimate by the number of feet of crack. We use the table below to establish an estimated volume of infiltration per foot of crack per hour.

TABLE 4-2. WINDOW INFILTRATION RATES

CLASS OF FIT	WINTER V/ HR × FT
Poor fit no weatherstripping, 3/32″ cracks............	200
Poor fit weatherstripping, 3/32″ cracks.................	90
Average fit no weatherstripping, 1/16″ cracks............	90
Average fit weatherstripping, 1/16″ cracks.................	50
Tight fit weatherstripping, 1/32″ cracks.................	30
Finest fit weatherstripping, 1/64″ cracks.................	10

When you survey your own windows for infiltration you will have to do some guessing about the dimensions of the cracks. You will not be able to measure the width of the cracks with accuracy. Pay particular attention to the cracks of movable sections. A running section is likely to have a poor or very poor fit. Note particularly the crack between the upper and lower sections of a double hung window. Cracks in these places are likely to be 3/32″ or larger. Try fitting a piece of paper in the crack. If you cannot, it is probably less than 1/32″. You are not likely to have a tight fit unless your window is quite new and has been designed especially for energy conservation.

Most engineering estimates neglect the putty or seal between glass and sash because they are dealing with new windows that manufacturers have sealed tightly. In established homes the seal can be important because of infiltration. Inspect the seal closely. If it is a putty seal, is it solid and evenly covered with paint, or are there granular places and pieces of putty missing? If the glass to sash seal is poor, downgrade your judgement of fit by one level.

These multipane colonial windows are interesting from an aesthetic point of view, but they can give you trouble in calculating your heat loss. You have about three times as much seal length as a one glass window. We suggest multiplying the crack length of a colonial window by 3 if the seal is poor.

Jalousie windows are unthinkable from an infiltration point of view. Not only are they always a loose fit, but also they have many times more linear feet of crack than any other type of window.

TRANSMISSION LOSSES

The air-to-air transmission loss for ordinary 1/8″ DS window glass is usually taken as U1.13, although you can find some manufacturers quoting slightly lower values. "Air-to-air" means that the surface resistance on both sides has been figured in. In summer the U value is usually taken as 1.06 because the wind velocity in summer is less than in winter, and the summer surface resistance is therefore greater.

The sash and casing of a window have characteristic loss rates, or U values, of their own. Instead of trying to compute the sash loss separately, engineers commonly apply an adjustment factor to the U value of the glass and calculate the heat loss for the entire window opening from the adjusted U value. Metal windows have a little higher adjustment factor than the wood sash type. Table 4-3 lists the adjusted U values we will use here. It is assumed that double and triple panes are glazed into the same sash.

TABLE 4-3.   ADJUSTED U VALUES

WINDOW TYPE	U VALUE	
	Wood Sash	*Metal Sash*
Single pane	1.15	1.27
Double pane, 1/4″ spacing	.59	.65
Double pane, 1/2″ or more spacing	.57	.63
Triple pane, 1/4″ spacing	.48	.53
Triple pane, 1/2″ or more spacing	.37	.40

YOUR WINDOW SURVEY

To take your window survey first make up a worksheet similar to Table 4-4.

Measure the square footage of window openings for each orientation and enter appropriately in the worksheet. The square footage must be entered according to orientation because the heat gain depends on the facing. Sash length and the IL and XL calculations may be entered according to orientation and the subtotals worked out and then added, or the

TABLE 4-4. WORKSHEET FOR WINDOW SURVEY

	N	E	SE	S	SW	W	TOTALS
Area							
Sash length							
U value							
Td							
Infiltration V							
IL							
XL							
IL + XL							
HG							
(IL + XL) − HG							
TOTALS							

entire area and length can be computed for IL and XL, whichever way you prefer. The U value is what you obtain from Table 4-3. Td is whatever you have decided to use for your own difference temperature between your thermostat and the local design temperature. You obtain HG by multiplying an appropriate number taken from Table 4-1 by the area of the windows in each orientation. Remember to apply the appropriate adjustment to E, SE, SW and W windows. NE and NW windows are counted as north windows, since the direct solar contributions to these orientations is virtually nil. Enter 0 as heat gain for the north windows, unless you feel optimistic and want to give some small credit to diffuse input, as we discussed above.

Since you will be using data from our previous tables, the answers you obtain will be in MBTU per heating season.

NOTE: Do not include glass in doors or patio doors in this worksheet. They will be covered in the next chapter.

FM HOME WINDOW LOSSES

We summarize in Tables 4-5 and 4-6 the transmission and infiltration losses for the windows of the FM homes to show how the numbers may work out for you. Remember that the FH homes have 130 linear feet of sash and 100 square feet of window opening distributed as 30 N, 15 E, 40 S, and 15 W. We assume the following conditions:

  □ Drafty class: single pane glass, poor fit windows, no weatherstripping

  □ Average class: single pane glass, poor fit, has weatherstripping

  □ Modern class: Storm windows or double pane glass, no weatherstripping

□ 90-75 class: not applicable. 90-75 lumps wall and window transmission
   losses into one specification
□ Superior class: storm windows or double pane glass to 3000 DD; triple
   pane above 3000 DD; average fit, weatherstripping
□ Ultra class: storm windows or double pane glass to 3000 DD; triple pane
   above 3000 DD; the owner has decided to reduce window area by 10
   square feet by filling in one north window with insulation in the winter; he
   uses insulating shutters above 3000 DD; finest fit with weatherstripping.

Note that Table 4-5 has a heat gain column. The heat gains are the same
regardless of the quality of the window, except for differences due to
latitude. They are also reduced when double pane or storm or triple pane
windows are used.

TABLE 4-5. WINDOW TRANSMISSION HEAT LOSS OF FM HOMES, MBTU

AU		115	115	60		40	36/18
HG	DD	DRAFTY	AVERAGE	MODERN	90-75	SUPERIOR	ULTRA
					Not		
9.2	1000	1.37	1.37	.716	applicable.	.716	.129
9.	2000	3.79	3.79	1.980	Windows	1.980	1.190
8.8	3000	6.53	6.53	3.410	are counted	3.410	2.050
8.6	4000	9.36	9.36	4.880	as part of	3.250	1.950
8.4	5000	12.71	12.71	6.620	wall.	4.420	2.650
8.3	6000	16.94	16.94	8.830		5.890	3.530
8.1	7000	21.74	21.74	11.340		7.560	4.540
7.9	8000	26.45	26.45	13.800		9.200	5.520
7.8	9000	31.21	31.21	16.280		10.860	6.510
7.5	10,000	98.39	98.39	19.360		12.900	7.740

TABLE 4-6. WINDOW INFILTRATION HEAT LOSS OF FM HOMES, MBTU

VU		468	211	211	70	70	21.6
Td	DD	DRAFTY	AVERAGE	MODERN	90-75	SUPERIOR	ULTRA
34	1000	5.58	2.52	2.52	.835	.835	.258
47	2000	15.40	6.95	6.95	2.310	2.310	.712
54	3000	26.60	11.98	11.98	3.980	3.980	1.230
58	4000	38.00	17.16	17.16	5.690	5.690	1.760
63	5000	51.70	23.29	23.29	7.730	7.730	2.870
70	6000	68.90	31.06	31.06	10.300	10.300	3.180
77	7000	88.50	39.88	39.88	13.230	13.230	4.080
82	8000	107.60	48.53	48.53	16.100	16.100	4.970
86	9000	127.00	57.27	57.27	19.000	19.000	5.860
92	10,000	151.00	68.07	68.07	22.580	22.580	6.970

To obtain net heat loss, or gain, add the values in Tables 4-5 and 4-6 and subtract the heat gain. These tables show that, if you really work hard on infiltration and make sure you have good storm windows, you can reduce your heat loss to the point where the gain is as much as or more than the heat loss, except in the coldest climates. In a 10,000 DD climate the heat gain advantages of good storm windows is only about 18%, but when you realize that the advantage is worth about $35 a year, it is not to be ignored.

UPGRADING YOUR WINDOWS

The steps you can take to upgrade your windows include caulking and weatherstripping, adding storm windows, replacing old windows with new, remodeling to achieve new window configurations, and modifying the interior shading effects.

Caulking and Weatherstripping

This upgrading step is one of the easiest and least expensive to apply and one of the most rewarding financially. Caulking and weatherstripping attacks the infiltration rate. Windows are a large source of this kind of heat loss. One of the nice things about caulking and weatherstripping is that they can bring the window infiltration factor all the way from Drafty to Superior without too much difficulty. All of the other factors require a substantial amount of effort to squeeze out the better refinements. Caulking and weatherstripping are jobs that almost anyone can do, so they should have a top priority on anyone's home improvement list.

Caulking refers to the application of some kind of plastic material to a crack for permanent application, and weatherstripping refers to the use of some kind of filler material at places that must opened, such as doors and windows. It often happens, however, that weatherstripping means both kinds of application.

Caulking compounds usually come in tubes, and application is by means of a caulking gun. The material is a soft, sticky plastic. It comes out of the tube through a nozzle, which must be cut off at the end before use. As you apply pressure to the gun you move the nozzle along a crack to be filled, and the caulk forms a bead. Caulking compound also comes in a rope bead. Use the finger to press it into cracks.

Caulking around window frames

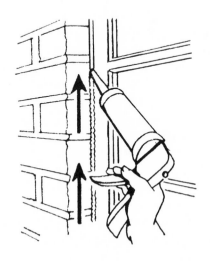

There are several types of caulking compound. They include:

- Oil or resin-based caulks. They will bond to wood masonry or metal
- Latex, butyl or polyvinyl-based caulks. They will bond to more surfaces and are more durable
- Silicone, polysulfide or polyurethane-based caulks. These elastometric caulks are more durable.

If you have extra wide cracks to fill, use oakum, caulking cotton, sponge rubber or glass fiber as a back-up before applying the caulk.

Places to caulk are:

- All around the edges of doors and windows where the frames meet the siding
- Where storm windows meet window frames, except drain holes at the bottom
- At corners formed by siding
- Around above-ground openings for water pipes and electric wires
- Where chimney or masonry meets the siding
- Where wires or pipes come through ceilings from an unheated attic
- Electric plug and switch boxes on outside walls.

Weatherstripping usually comes in strips of matted fiber. It is usually applied at door openings. The best way to apply it is to add a strip of wood to the door jamb and tack the weatherstripping to the strip so that when the door closes there will be a snug fit between fiber and door.

Doors may also be weatherstripped by the use of springy metal strips nailed to the inside of the door jamb. When the door is closed, the springy metal presses against the edge of the door and reduces the air leakage.

Temporary or seasonal weatherstripping can be applied to windows that open in summer. Sealing tape such as is used on heat pipes by the people who install ductwork can be applied to the cracks of double hung windows. The rope type caulking compound makes a good sealer for these cracks.

Remember that the purpose of caulking and weatherstripping is to make infiltration cracks air tight. There is some amount of pressure difference between the inside and outside caused by the wind and the temperature differences. Where there is pressure, air comes in even through the smallest crack. Our aim is to fill these cracks tight enough to resist the

pressure. Caulking on the side of the prevailing wind is essentially important because in winter the cold wind can easily be over 25 mph, causing
considerable air pressure.

Benefits

In Table 4-7 we summarize the savings you can obtain by adding
caulking and weatherstripping to two classes of windows. The numbers
are impressive. For example, upgrading a poor fit window in a 6000 DD
climate will save .29 MBTU, or $1.46, per linear foot of crack.If you
have 100 feet of sash, you save $146 per season in fuel bills. If you
upgrade an average fit window the savings will be .106 MBTU, or $53
per season.

TABLE 4-7. SAVINGS FROM UPGRADED WINDOWS

DD	UPGRADING FROM POOR FIT		UPGRADING FROM AVERAGE FIT	
	MBTU	$	MBTU	$
1000	.049	.24	.018	.09
2000	.097	.49	.035	.18
3000	.150	.73	.053	.27
4000	.195	.97	.071	.35
5000	.243	1.22	.088	.44
6000	.292	1.46	.106	.53
7000	.340	1.70	.124	.62
8000	.390	1.94	.141	.71
9000	.438	2.19	.160	.80
10,000	.486	2.43	.177	.90

Upgrading with Storm Windows

Those who preach energy conservation have two songs, insulate
attics and install storm windows. Good advice, if you know what you are
doing. Reference to Table 4-8 will enable you to calculate your savings,
using the familiar equation,

$$XL = A \times U \times Td \times 24 \times .95 \times DD/65.$$

You simply determine the XL for your present window, using $U = 1.15$
for a single wood window, 1.27 for a single metal window, .57 for a
double wood, or .63 for a double metal. Then calculate the XL for the
storm combinations of Table 4-8 and subtract the two.

TABLE 4-8.   U VALUE OF PRIME AND STORM WINDOW
COMBINATIONS

TYPE	SINGLE PRIME PLUS STORM	DOUBLE PRIME PLUS STORM
Wood prime, wood storm	.58	.38
Wood prime, metal storm	.60	.39
Metal prime, metal storm	.63	.42

The infiltration leakage rate for storm windows is the same as for prime windows; that is, the rate depends on the class of fit. In older homes the storm window is often the hung-on type. If well-fitted and weatherstripped, this type probably has the leakage rate of a loose, non-weatherstripped, double hung window. Moveable metal storm windows, if caulked, probably have an average fit. Refer to Table 4-2.

If the prime and storm window each have the same leakage rate, the combined rate is about 70% of the prime rate alone. If a fairly tight storm window is fitted over a loose prime, the infiltration rate is about 50% of the prime.

There will be less heat gain through windows fitted with storms. Remember that the transmittance of visible light is about 86% of the full value because of the losses due to reflection and absorption. Since the storm window adds another sheet of glass, the heat gain is reduced by about 14%. Recall that Table 4-1 lists the heat gain for double glass in the last column. This column can be used to determine the heat gain of a single prime with storm combination. If you have a triple sheet combination, you must multiply the last column of Table 4-1 to get the heat gain.

In recent years many homes have been built with double pane prime windows. This feature appears to offer the householder the opportunity to get the benefit of storm windows without bother of hanging them every fall. This window does indeed cut the XL losses in half, but the IL losses are those of a single window. Remember that storm windows can give a 30% to 50% improvement on infiltration losses. This window probably has the leakage characteristics of an average fit with weatherstripping. If you live in a 6000 DD climate or colder you should consider putting storm windows over the double windows that are on the north side. They will save you about 30% of the heat loss of the double windows. In most cases you would not consider putting triple windows on the south because the extra pane would reduce the heat gain.

To determine the cost effectiveness of storm windows, recalculate your worksheet using the new U values and infiltration rates. Convert the seasonal Btu's obtained to dollars and note how much you save with storm windows. In a 6000 DD climate you will probably find a saving of about $8.50 per season for a single glass $3' \times 4'$ window. If you can buy a new storm window for about $30 to $40 your payback period will be from 3 1/2 to 5 years.

You have probably heard of putting a sheet of plastic over a window on the outside as a kind of cheap storm window. How effective is it? The transmission resistance of a sheet of plastic is 0. If the sheet can be tightly fitted and extended over the frame the infiltration losses will be reduced. A tight fit will also reduce the wind effect and hence will increase the surface resistance of the glass. There is some benefit from a plastic sheet, but not much is known about the quantitative effects.

Window Replacement

You may be hit with the remodeling bug to the point where you want to replace those old windows completely. You may wish a more modern style, or you may despair that those rotting, warped, poor-fitting windows can be repaired enough to work any real energy savings. Very poor fitting windows may have a leakage rate much higher than the maximum 200 cubic feet per hour that we have used in our basis figures.

If you replace windows, we suggest that you provide nothing less than the double pane type. It is not worth spending money for installation unless you buy the extra pane of glass.

We could review the different types of windows available, but it will actually be more profitable for you to go directly to the tradesmen themselves. We should call your attention to two innovations that are worth considering. One is the vinyl cladding now offered on wood windows. This feature eliminates the need for paint and reduces the moisture damage to the wood. The other innovation is the thermal barrier on metal frames. One big objection to metal windows is that the sash is such a good conductor of heat. Remember from our earlier discussion that the adjustment factor for a wood frame raises the U value of a window from the nominal U 1.13 for glass to U 1.15. But the adjusted U value for the metal window is 1.27. The adjustment factor for a metal window with a thermal barrier is 1, meaning that you count only the glass U when computing. The thermal barrier is a piece of highly resistant plastic separating the sash member touching the outside air and the sash member touching the inside air.

When you start talking with vendors you will be offered a number of choices and some conflicting claims. Remember, there are only three factors affecting the performance of glass windows:

□ The properties of the glass: Its transmittance. Its reflectance. Its heat gain. These properties will not vary with any great significance among the types of glass you will want. Do not be misled into choosing special glass, such as heat absorbing or tinted types unless you have become prepared to know that these are what you need. Such special glass is sometimes designed into large buildings to reduce air conditioning load, but it is seldom offered for residential use.

□ The choice of wood or metal sash.

□ The factor of infiltration, which is a function of the construction of the window, the frame and the skill of the tradesmen who install it.

If you are remodeling an old building to the point of changing the exterior lines, new windows are of course quite proper. However, it hardly pays to replace windows just to make them more energy efficient, unless they are beyond repair. Usually, repairs and storm windows are the only upgrading features that are economically practical. If you do replace, choose a quality product. Avoid at all effort the choice of the do-it-yourself window available at the usual builders supply store.

Upgrading with Shades and Drapes

The architect and builder go to great lengths to ensure plenty of window area. Lots of light and visibility are good sales features. Witness the popularity of the ''picture window.''

Given lots of window area the homemaker and interior decorator immediately proceed to cut back on the light and visibility with shades and drapes, pleading the aesthetic argument. These devices are not wrong; they are right for the wrong reasons. They deplete the very qualities offered by a large glass area.

The error in the use of shades and drapes is our failure to recognize them for their potential control over heat transmission. Unfortunately, so little research has been done by either the heating engineer or the interior decorator that there is very little information to report. It is only recently that the importance of blocking heat escape from windows has begun to gain widespread attention.

At the same time that the sun is inducing heat gain through a window in the winter, heat is escaping by conduction through the glass. Even on the coldest days, however, the solar input, while the sun is shining, exceeds the conductance loss. At night or on heavy days of dark clouds there is no solar input and only transmission loss. It would be very helpful if, at those times, there were some way to insulate the glass. We would like to have something as effective as wall insulation when needed, yet transparent to sunlight when needed. Solar engineers have come to call this something moveable insulation because the only way to meet the specifications at present is to move a piece of insulation over the window at night and remove it during the day.

Solar engineers do not recognize conventional shades and drapes as moveable insulation because they do not provide the true equivalence of genuine insulation. However, these materials are not totally without merit. A study at the Illinois Institute of Technology showed that roller shades over a single pane window could reduce heat loss by 28%, venetian blinds by 7% and drapes by 6%. Until more definitive information has been developed by experiment, you can use these percentages to adjust your window heat loss estimates.

Light colored shades and drapes are better than dark because they reflect heat back into the room. Vertical louver shades are better than venetian blinds because they offer better control over glare.

One of the serious unknowns is quantitative information about the relative effectiveness of different types of drapery materials. It seems reasonable that heavy, close weave, lined drapes should be more effective against heat transmission than light, loose weave type, but how much more we do not know.

Solar heating enthusiasts have devised a very simple kind of moveable insulation. If you can learn to live the simple life and return to doing things by hand, you will find it very effective. The technique is to cut a piece of insulating board just the size of the inside of the window frame and press it against the glass. It is important that this material press the glass closely because a close press can cut down on infiltration losses as well as on transmission losses. Put the insulation board into the window at night and remove it in the morning. Or, put it in a north window all winter, if you wish. Some people have used 2-inch thick polystyrene, which is an ideal choice, except that it gives off a noxious gas if it burns.

The one ideally perfect moveable insulation goes by the trade name "Beadwall." This material consists of loose polystyrene beads $1/8''$ to $3/16''$ in diameter. The window for this application has two panes of glass separated by 2 to 4 inches of air space. The beads can be moved from place to place by means of a blower. When you desire to insulate the window, the beads are blown or pumped into the air space. When you want the window clear, the beads are sucked out of the air space and dumped into a storage container. The insulating value of Beadwall is U .3 per inch. The thicker the air space the better the U value. One nice advantage of the Beadwall system is that it can be controlled by automatic operation of the pumps.

Although Beadwall seems an ideal solution. there are a number of technical problems. After a few cycles it was found that the beads accumulated static and tended to cling to the glass, ducts and containers. This problem was solved by coating the beads with an anti-static agent. Another problem is pressure within the air space developed by the pumps. The panels must be vented to relieve the pressure, and just ordinary glass cannot be used because it will not stand the pressure in case the vents become accidentally plugged. The glass-to-casing seal must be perfect to exclude water because water would be worse than static in restricting the movement of the beads. In short, installation of Beadwall is not a job for the do-it-yourselfer.

Beadwall installation costs from $3 to $10 per square foot, depending on the complexity of the situation. It should pay for itself in fuel savings in less than 10 years.

"Insealshaid" is the trade name of another commercial product that has attacked the problem of heat loss, and gain, through windows. The device is a snuggly fitting box attached inside the window frame in the interior of the house. Within the box are three patented "shaids" that can be rolled up like conventional roller shades. The shaid facing the room consists of material having a 44% visibility. The opaque portion of this shaid is blackened on the side facing the window so as to absorb solar energy. This shaid is called the collector. The middle shaid, which is 1" from the collector shaid, is of clear plastic. Solar energy causes heat to build up in the space between the collector and the middle shaid. There are louvers at the bottom and top of the box connecting this air space and the room. The openings are thermostatically controlled. When the upper part of the air space reaches 82 degrees, the louvers open and heated air from the window circulates into the room. The third shaid, the one closest to the window, is coated to reflect a portion of the sunlight. The collector and middle shaid are raised in summer and the reflective shaid lowered to reduce summer heat gain. In winter the reflective shaid should be lowered at night and raised in the day. Drapes can be used over this device if they are installed in a way that will not interfere with the louvers.

The makers claim a U value of .31 for Insealshaid in the two-shaid heating mode and .18 in the three-shaid night configuration. They claim an infiltration reduction of 2/3 that of an average fit weatherstripped window. They estimate the cost of home size windows at $4 to $7 per square foot plus installation. They also point out that their collector shaid is able to develop heat even with diffuse light on cloudy days.

Devices such as Insealshaid restrict the amount of visibility, although the amount is not objectionable for most purposes. They also restrict the amount of solar energy entering a room, which means that there is less visible light to be converted to infrared by absorption in the floors, walls and furniture. However, we suggest that the conversion efficiency is probably better than that of floors, walls and furniture.

One of the greatest needs in the energy field is an effective, inexpensive, practical moveable insulation for the retrofit market. Many ideas have been suggested, but most of them are either impractical or have been custom designed for a particular situation. We may expect American inventive genius to do something about it. You would do well to keep your eyes open for such devices if you are not ready to upgrade your windows.

Sources for insulating drapes and shades are: Insealshaid, P.O. Box 428, Butler, WI; Appropriate Technology Corporation, P.O. Box 975, Brattleboro, VT 05301. Glass information can be obtained from PPG Industries, Inc., One Gateway Center, Pittsburgh, PA 15222. Solar collector glazing information can be obtained from Kalwall Corporation, Solar Components Division, P.O. Box 237, Manchester, NH 03105.

5

What To Do About Doors

THE XL LOSS OF DOORS

The transmission heat loss of doors can be calculated from the R values given in Table 5-1.

TABLE 5-1. R VALUES OF VARIOUS DOORS

TYPE	DOOR ONLY	INSIDE AIR TO OUTSIDE AIR	INSIDE AIR TO STORM
Solid, hardwood, 2" thick	1.82	2.67	3.18
Solid, hardwood 1 3/4" thick	1.59	2.44	2.95
Paneled, softwood, 1 1/4" thick	1.56	2.41	2.92
Hollow	1.50	2.50	2.86

If your doors are combinations of both wood and glass, the heat loss for each portion should be computed separately and added.

THE IL LOSS OF DOORS

It is very difficult to prevent infiltration from doors. By the nature of a door it is inclined to have a loose fit, and, after use, it probably has a very loose fit. The leakage rate will probably be over 200 cubic feet per hour per linear foot of crack on the windward side, unless you take special precautions. If you weatherstrip all cracks and attach a door sweep to both the inside and outside of the door bottom, you may succeed in getting the infiltration rate down to 100 cubic feet per hour. For our computations we will use 200 cubic feet per hour per linear foot of crack for the worst case and 100 cubic feet per hour for the case of good weatherstripping.

SLIDING GLASS DOORS

Sliding glass doors have a U value of .56 if the frame is wood, or .58 if the frame is metal. When the doors are new, they probably have a fit equivalent to average with weatherstripping, or 50 cubic feet per hour per linear foot of the perimeter of the door. After a few years of use they are probably equivalent to an average fit without weatherstripping, or 90 cubic feet per hour.

INFILTRATION FROM OPEN DOORS

It is impossible to give a general estimate of the amount of air that gets in through open doors. If your door opens directly to the outside, there is no wind, and you close the door quickly, about 100 cubic feet of cold air may get in. If there is a strong wind blowing, the penetration may be 10 times that amount. If you have a large, active family, the door might be opened more than 50 times a day (and closed slowly in many cases). If your family consists of two not very active persons, or persons who are away at work all day, the door may be opened very little. We estimate that in a 6000 DD climate and average mild wind and about 20 openings a day the seasonal cost of fuel would be about $25. But with an average strong wind and an active family it might cost $250 a year.

UPGRADING BY CUTTING BACK

You can always spend less by using less. You can spend less on fuel by setting back your thermostat. You can spend less heat loss through windows by blocking up some of them. In the case of doors, you can lose less heat by blocking up one or more of them.

Many homes have three or more outside doors, but only one gets most family use. One or more of these doors could be blocked off with insulation. There are two ways to do it. If there is a storm door, the space between the prime and storm could be filled with bat type insulation, closing the edges against infiltration with sealing tape. Otherwise, a panel of insulating board could be fitted over the inside of the door, letting it extend over the door jamb and fastening it along the edges with sealing tape.

You should always keep two doors clear and workable for your own protection and to comply with fire laws. Therefore, if you have only two doors, you should not use this cut-back method of reducing heat loss. Note, however, that blocking the doors with insulation in the way described would not prevent you from exiting through them in an emergency.

UPGRADING WITH STORM DOORS

If you do not have storm doors, you need to start thinking about them right away.

If you have storm doors that were installed within the last 20 years, they probably are combination screen and storm doors where you convert to storm by replacing the screen with glass. If you start looking for storm doors now, that is probably the first kind you will be offered.

Let us see what such a storm door does for us. These doors are mostly glass, except for an aluminum kickplate a foot or so wide at the bottom. The transmission resistance of this plate is virtually zero. In effect, this plate reduces the resistance by about 20%. The effective U value of the door opening becomes about 1.42.

We determine the U value of the prime and storm combination by adding each of the resistances and taking the reciprocal:

1 3/4″ solid hardwood door	2.95	
Storm door	.70	
Total	3.65	U value = .27

Note that the resistance of the prime door is increased by about 24% by this aluminum-glass storm.

The infiltration qualities of this door are very poor. The junction of the door and the frame constitute one set of cracks, and the junction of the glass and the frame constitute another set of almost equal length. Both of these sets are very loose and without weatherstripping, so the air leakage is probably well over 200 cubic feet per hour. We have no evidence that the infiltration of this door combination has ever been measured. We suspect, however, that the storm door brings little, if any, improvement to the infiltration of the prime door. If the prime has a leakage rate of 200 cubic feet per hour, it probably still has close to that amount with the storm door.

Heavy, 2″ aluminum storm doors with about 40% glass and with R7 insulation between the aluminum skins are available. Such a door would have an adjusted U value of about .21, giving a combination U value with a solid wood door of about .13. The cracks of this door could be weatherstripped so that the infiltration could be brought down to 100 cubic feet per hour. Following the rule that, if the storm and the prime have about the same infiltration, the rate of the prime is cut by 50%, the combination of solid prime and quality storm could cut the infiltration of the prime to 50 cubic feet per hour.

VESTIBULES, BREEZEWAYS, PORCHES

Most people assume that you can cure the ills of a door exposed to the elements by building a vestibule around it. Surprisingly, it can be demonstrated that the transmission loss into a vestibule is no better than a quality storm and prime house door, and sometimes it is poorer.

One way to see why this apparent contradiction is true is to take a look at Table 3-1 and note that as the ceiling insulation gets better the attic temperature gets closer to the outside temperature. The reason is easy to guess. The more heat loss into the attic the higher the attic temperature.

The same situation prevails with a vestibule. The better the house door the more nearly the vestibule temperature approaches the outside temperature. But people are complacent if they have a vestibule. They assume that no special precautions have to be taken on the house door because they have a vestibule. However, temperature transmission through the common house door reaches an equilibrium between the house temperature and the outside temperature. This equilibrium tends to follow, as a seasonal average, the Td temperature, if the house door is the common type without weatherstripping. That is, the Td in the vestibule is about the same as the Td derived by the conventional DD methods. The house door faces about the same Td with a vestibule as it does without! The only way to overcome the heat loss into the vestibule is to install a quality storm and prime house door, an action which the vestibule was supposed to avoid.

We see a different picture, however, when we look at infiltration loss. Remember there are two sources of infiltration loss, open door penetration and crack penetration. Low open door penetration with rapid closings in little or no wind may cause 100 cubic feet per opening. At 20 openings a day, a least case situation may produce 2000 cubic feet per day of infiltration. With a slow closing in a strong wind the penetration could be 1000 cubic feet per opening. At 50 openings per day, the worst case situation would be 50,000 cubic feet per day. A high rate of crack infiltration, characterized by a poor fitting door and no weatherstripping, would be 200 cubic feet per hour per linear foot of crack. A normal rate, characterized by weatherstripping, would be 100 cubic feet per hour, and a low rate, characterized by a quality storm door with good weatherstripping, would be 50 cubic feet per hour.

Now, if we put a vestibule around this door, and ensure that the vestibule is tight and has a quality storm door and is large enough that the outside door will always be closed before the inner door is opened, then we have eliminated a large part of the wind pressure effect upon infiltration and are left with pressure caused by temperature difference as the main cause of infiltration through cracks. We estimate that the infiltration with a vestibule would be 30% of what it would be without a vestibule. This estimate is our educated guess. The fact that we cannot give you any better number is an indication of the gaps that must be filled yet before we can confidently and intelligently design or retrofit a building for conservation and solar energy.

A glance at the numbers is impressive. Table 5-2 shows the infiltration losses for the FM homes. Any of these doors can be reduced by 75% by building a vestibule around it. (The Ultra class has had this reduction already taken.) Consider the drafty home in the 6000 DD climate. One door (Table 5-2 is for two doors) could be reduced from an infiltration loss of 10.1 MBTU to 2.5 MBTU with a vestibule. Table 5-2 shows only the loss from crack penetration. It does not include the open door penetra-

TABLE 5-2.   INFILTRATION LOSSES OF FM DOORS, MBTU

Td	VU	68.3	68.4	34.2	25.6	17.1	5.3
	DD	DRAFTY	AVERAGE	MODERN	90-75	SUPERIOR	ULTRA
34	1000	1.63	1.63	.82	.61	.41	.09
47	2000	4.50	4.50	2.30	1.60	1.13	.28
54	3000	7.80	7.80	3.90	3.03	1.90	.49
58	4000	11.10	11.10	5.60	4.20	2.80	.71
63	5000	15.10	15.10	7.60	5.70	3.80	.99
70	6000	20.20	20.20	10.10	7.70	5.00	1.34
77	7000	25.90	25.90	12.90	9.70	6.50	1.70
82	8000	31.50	31.50	15.70	11.80	7.90	2.10
86	9000	37.00	37.00	18.60	13.90	9.30	2.50
92	10,000	44.00	44.00	22.00	16.60	11.00	3.10

tion because that loss is so much a product of life style it cannot be predicted. However, if we take the assumed least case, we find that the seasonal open door loss would be about 5.3 MBTU; then, if we assume again that the vestibule would reduce infiltration by 75%, the enclosed door loss would be 1.33 MBTU. Or, the worst case would be reduced from an amazing 42.6 MBTU to 10.7 MBTU.

If the homeowners were to combine the 7 MBTU savings from the Drafty crack infiltration with the 30 MBTU saving from the worst case door open penetration, he would save $185 a year in heating costs. That amount would pay for the building of a vestibule. However, if he owned the Modern class in the 6000 DD climate and combined the 1.5 MBTU savings for crack penetration with the 1.6 MBTU savings for the least case door open penetration, the yearly savings in dollars would be only $15. In fact, the home owner who could spend $185 might find better ways of doing it.

The vestibule can be an energy benefit to you if you build it to Superior class conservation and incorporate solar collection and storage facilities according to the principles discussed in Chapter 9. If you add enough solar heat to the vestibule to maintain a seasonal average somewhat above the DD average, your house door heat loss will be substantially reduced. For example, if you maintain a vestibule temperature 20 degrees above the DD average, your savings will amount to about 48% of what you would normally lose through the house door. (Average class door in a 6000 DD climate.)

The same 48% saving would result if you used a Superior class door in a solar heated vestibule. The conclusion is that, if you can add solar heat to the vestibule in sufficient quantity, you do not need an expensive house door. However, if you do not add heat to the vestibule, you must upgrade the house door just as if the vestibule were not there.

The comments about vestibules apply also to enclosed breezeways and porches.

There are motivations other than conservation that justify the addition of a vestibule or enclosure of a breezeway or porch. You may need a mud room or additional closet space. Enclosed breezeways and porches temper the summer sun and make pleasant places to relax on a summer evening. We do suggest that when one of these home improvements are added they be built to Superior class conservation standards. You may not see the need for including solar heat in the addition right now, but the time will surely come when this high quality construction will pay off.

FM DOOR HEAT LOSSES

The infiltration heat loss and transmission heat loss are summarized in Tables 5-2 and 5-3. The FM homes have two doors, each with an area of 19.5 square feet and a perimeter of 19 feet. The Ultra home, however, uses only one door in winter. They have incorporated insulation into the door in such a way as to get the U value down to .13 and the air leakage rate down to 15 cubic feet per hour, but the door can still be opened easily in an emergency.

TABLE 5-3. TRANSMISSION LOSSES OF FM DOORS, MBTU

	AU	8.09	7.99	5.27		2.5	2.5
Td	DD	DRAFTY	AVERAGE	MODERN	90–75	SUPERIOR	ULTRA
34	1000	.2	.19	.13		.06	.3
47	2000	.5	.50	.30	Not	.20	.3
54	3000	.9	.90	.60	Applicable.	.30	.3
58	4000	1.3	1.30	.90	Part of	.40	.3
63	5000	1.8	1.80	1.20	Wall.	.60	.3
70	6000	2.4	2.40	1.60		.70	.3
77	7000	3.0	3.00	2.00		.90	.3
82	8000	3.7	3.70	2.40		1.20	.3
86	9000	4.4	4.30	2.80		1.40	.3
92	10,000	5.2	5.10	3.40		1.60	.3

These doors have the following characteristics:

- Drafty: Paneled softwood 1 1/4", loose fit, no storm door, no weatherstripping, 200 ft^3 leakage
- Average: Solid hardwood 1 3/4", loose fit, ordinary storm door, no weatherstripping, 200 ft^3 leakage
- Modern: Solid hardwood 1 3/4", average fit, ordinary storm door, weatherstripping, 100 ft^3 leakage
- Superior: Solid hardwood 2", average fit, quality storm door, weatherstripping, 50 ft^3 leakage
- Ultra: Same as Superior but with heated vestibule.

When we examine these tables we are again struck by the dramatic reduction in loss that can be achieved by attention to infiltration. Note in Table 5-2 the saving of 10 MBTU, or 50%, between the Average home and the Modern home in the 6000 DD climate. This saving is almost entirely due to weatherstripping. Note the additional 50% reduction between the Modern home and the Superior home when a quality storm window with greatly improved leakage protection replaces an ordinary leaky glass-aluminum storm door.

But when we compare the cost versus the saving we are confronted with a moral dilemma common to energy conservation and conversion desires. The energy saving between the ordinary storm door and the quality door in a 6000 DD climate is about 5 MBTU, or $25. That $25 would pay for an ordinary storm door in two years, while it would probably take 6 years to pay off the quality storm door at the same rate. We may question whether the superior door is economically justified.

In fact, we may even question whether any storm door is economically justified, especially below about 3000 degree days. Then we must remember that sometimes there are value-added features having no economic worth. There are aesthetic values and sense-of-pride values that have meaning only to the individual, not to the market place. One of these values is the desire to have things of better quality, knowing they will be cheaper in the long run.

One of the strongest motivations from the viewpoint we are stressing here is the desire to move the home into the Superior class of energy efficiency if at all possible. As we shall soon see, if we can get our home into at least that class, we open up a new world of energy management. From this viewpoint, every Btu saved gets us that much closer to our goal. Paying a little extra for a Btu here sometimes makes sense in the larger picture because it may help to save several Btu's there.

Some good contacts for further information are: National Solar Heating and Cooling Information Center, P.O. Box 1607, Rockville, MD 20850 (phone: 800-523-2929; In Pennsylvania, 800-426-4983); Energy Research and Development Administration, Office of Public Affairs, Washington, DC 20545; ERDA Technical Information Center, P.O. Box 62, Oak Ridge, TN 37830; U.S. Department of Housing and Urban Development, Washington, DC; National Association of Home Builders Research Foundation, Inc., P.O. Box 1627, Rockville, MD 20850.

6

What To Do
About Walls

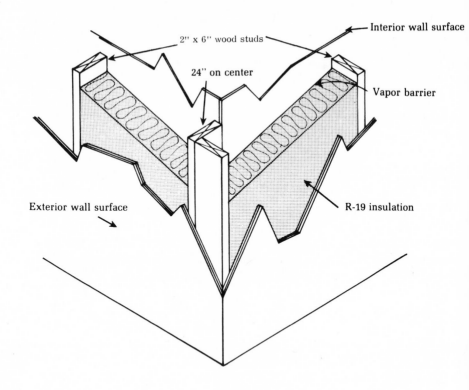

2" x 6" wood studs

24" on center

Interior wall surface

Vapor barrier

Exterior wall surface

R-19 insulation

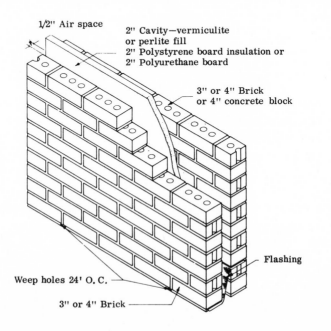

1/2" Air space

2" Cavity—vermiculite
or perlite fill

2" Polystyrene board insulation or
2" Polyurethane board

3" or 4" Brick
or 4" concrete block

Flashing

Weep holes 24' O.C.

3" or 4" Brick

SURVEYING YOUR WALLS

The first thing to do about the walls of your home is to determine how many square feet are exposed to the weather and how many are exposed to an interior space, such as an enclosed breezeway or garage. Do not include the above grade basement wall in your measurements. You may have to go back to your grade school arithmetic to compute the area of the triangles in the gables. Remember the rule? Area of a triangle equals the base times one-half the altitude. After you have determined the gross area of wall, subtract the area of windows and doors to obtain the net area.

Next, you have to try to figure out what constitutes the layers of your wall. Determining the material of the layers is not easy. Much of it has to be guesswork. There are certain standard ways to build a wall, and you will probably have to assume your construction from these standards.

The frame house probably has the following layers: Exterior siding or shingles, building paper, sheathing boards or plywood 3/4" thick, 2" × 4" studs, insulation (maybe), vapor barrier as part of the insulation or separate (maybe), and lath and plaster or gypsum board.

Masonry walls involve you in even bigger guesswork. They come in so many varieties. For example: Face brick over stud walls; solid brick; concrete block; combinations of brick and concrete block; with or without exterior stucco; with or without interior plaster. The density of masonry has a lot to do with its U value, and you have no way of determining what that density is unless you have access to the original specifications. The thickness of masonry walls may vary from 6 to 12 inches. The wall may be solid, or there may be a cavity of perhaps 2 inches between the exterior and interior layer.

It is very important that you know whether you have insulation in the walls, but it may not be easy to find out. In a frame house you may be able to tell by removing the box of a wall electrical plug or switch and looking or feeling back of it. If you find any, you may not even then be able to tell the R value. If it is a 2" bat of fiberglass or mineral wool, it will be R7. If it is bat type and fills the entire stud, it will be R11. If it is foam, it will proabably be about R15. Sometimes you can judge by inference. For example, if the builder put R7 in the attic, he probably used only R7, if any, in the sidewalls.

Masonry insulation is even more difficult to identify. There may or may not be insulation in the cavity, if there is one. Loose insulation may have been poured into the cells of concrete block. A foam-type insulation contractor may be willing to do an exploratory drilling for you. There seems no other way to find out what you have, unless you happen to know the builder and can trust his memory.

WALL R VALUES

We list in Table 6-1 the R value of most of the common building materials. To find the total R value you simply add the R values of each layer of the wall. Remember that to calculate the total air-to-air resistance of a wall you must also include the outside and inside surface resistance, which, for interior air, is .68 and, for exterior winter air, is .17. Example:

Outside air	.17	
Siding	.81	
Sheathing	.94	
Insulation	7.00	
Gypsum board	.32	
Inside air	.68	
Total	9.92	$U = 1/9.92 = 1$

TABLE 6-1.   R VALUES OF BUILDING MATERIALS

BOARD		Insulating sheathing,	
		1/2"	1.32
Wood, softwood, 3/4"	.94	3/4"	2.06
per inch	1.25		
Wood, hardwood,		INSULATION	
3/4"	.74		
per inch	.94	Fiberglass, per inch,	
Plywood, 1/4"	.31	bat or loose	3.70
3/8"	.47	Mineral wool, per	
1/2"	.63	inch, bat or	
5/8"	.78	loose	3.70
3/4"	.94	Cellulose, per inch,	
Wood fiber hard-		loose	3.70
board, 1/4"	.18	Vermiculite, per	
		inch	2.12
SIDING		Perlite, per inch	2.56
		Rigid fiberglass	
Wood shingles	.87	board, per inch	4.00
Wood lap siding	.81		

TABLE 6-1 (continued)

Polystyrene board, per inch	5.00	Linoleum	.08
Polyurethane board, per inch	6.25	Terrazzo, ceramic	.08
Urea foam, per inch	5.25	Carpet, foam rubber pad	1.23
Outside air, winter	.17	PLASTER	
summer	.25	Gypsum board, 3/8″	.32
Air space, 3/4″ to 4″	.97	1/2″	.45
with bright foil lining	3.08	Gypsum plaster, sand aggregate	.09
BUILDING PAPER		Gypsum plaster, light weight aggregate	.32
Felt	.06	Cement plaster, sand aggregate	.10
Asphalt roll	.15	Stucco, per inch	.20
Vapor seal, plastic	0.00	MASONRY	
ROOFING		Concrete block*	
Wood shingles	.94	sand & gravel 8″	1.11
Asphalt shingles	.44	sand & gravel 12″	1.28
Asbestos shingles	.21	cinder 8″	1.72
Slate	.05	cinder 12″	1.89
Sheet metal	0.00	Poured concrete per inch	.08
FLOORING		Brick, face, per inch	.11
Vinyl tile	.05	common, per inch	.20
Asphalt tile	.04	Stone, per inch	.08
Rubber tile	.02		
Cork tile	.28		

*NOTE: These values are quoted by HUD in "Minimum Design Standards for Heat Loss Calculation." The National Concrete Masonry Association provides different values based on density of the concrete per cubic foot. Since you have no way of knowing the density of your concrete, the HUD numbers are easier to apply.

In order to help you determine the approximate transmission coefficient of your walls we have listed in Table 6-2 the R values of common types of walls.

TABLE 6-2. R VALUES OF SEVERAL TYPICAL WALLS

FRAME	
Lap siding, building paper, wood sheathing, gypsum board	
no insulation	4.08
2″ insulation	10.11
3 1/2″ insulation	14.11
Shingles, 1/2″ insulating sheathing, gypsum board	
no insulation	4.53
2″ insulation	10.56
3 1/2″ insulation	14.56
MASONRY	
Brick Veneer	
Face brick, 1/2″ insulating sheathing, 2″ × 4″ furring, gypsum board	
no insulation	4.03
2″ insulation	10.06
3 1/2″ insulation	14.06

TABLE 6-2 (continued)

All Masonry

Face brick 4″, common brick 4″, 1″, furring, gypsum board		3.51
Single wythe 6″ solid brick, 1″ furring, gypsum board		
no insulation		2.94
1″ polystyrene sheathing		6.25
Single wythe 6″ or 8″ hollow brick, 1″ furring, gypsum board		
no insulation		3.33
1″ polystyrene sheathing		6.66
Vermiculite-filled cores		5.00
Perlite filled cores		5.26
foam filled cores		6.25
Composite, 4″ brick, 4″ concrete block, 1″ furring, gypsum board		
no insulation		4.16
1″ polystyrene sheathing		6.33

Brick & concrete block, 8″, no finish

	Sand & Gravel	Cinder
no insulation	1.11	1.72
loose fill in cores	2.25	2.68
no insulation, gypsum board		
on furring strips	2.61	3.23
no insulation, foil-backed		
gypsum on furring	4.65	5.26
loose fill, gypsum board		
on furring strips	3.56	4.17
loose fill, foil-backed gypsum		
on furring strips	5.64	6.25
1″ rigid fiberglass, gypsum		
board	5.27	5.88
same with loose filled cores	6.53	7.14
1″ polystyrene, gypsum		
board	6.53	7.14

If exterior finished with stucco, add R .20.

Sometimes a basic wall described in Table 6-2 has been ''improved'' over the years with an exterior addition. For example, it was quite common a few years back to put asphalt shingles over wood siding. If such is the case with your home, simply add the R value of asphalt shingles to the R value of the frame wall found in Table 6-2. Examples are even known of aluminum siding being placed over asphalt shingles, which were placed over wood siding.

XL WALL LOSSES

In Table 6-3 we list the probable transmission losses for the FM homes. After you have computed your own wall loss, compare it with Table 6-3. Remember that to make this comparison you have to determine the ratio between your wall area and the area of the FM wall. Recall that the net FM wall area is 1034 square feet. Suppose that your own wall area is 1232 square feet. Then, $1034/1232 = .84$ is your decimal multiplier. Suppose you calculate your wall loss to be 42.3 MBTU. Then, $42.3 \times .84 = 35.53$. Table 6-3 shows the FM wall loss to be 34.32 for the Average FM home in a 6000 DD climate. If you have decided that your home belongs in the Average class, your wall is losing about 1 MBTU more than the standard. Have you gaged your AU factor correctly?

TABLE 6-3. TRANSMISSION LOSSES OF FM WALLS, MBTU

AU		253	233	99		71	30
Td	DD	DRAFTY	AVERAGE	MODERN	90-75	SUPERIOR	ULTRA
34	1000	3.0	2.8	1.2	4.10	.85	.36
47	2000	8.6	7.7	3.3	10.10	2.30	.99
54	3000	14.7	13.2	5.6	17.41	4.00	1.70
58	4000	20.6	19.0	8.0	23.80	5.80	2.40
63	5000	27.9	25.7	10.9	30.20	7.80	3.30
70	6000	37.3	34.3	14.6	37.70	10.50	4.40
77	7000	47.8	44.0	18.7	44.90	13.40	5.70
82	8000	58.2	53.6	22.8	51.20	16.30	6.90
86	9000	68.7	63.2	26.9	55.30	19.30	8.10
92	10,000	81.6	75.2	31.9	60.40	22.90	9.70

INFILTRATION THROUGH WALLS

There may be considerable infiltration through the walls of a home. Unfortunately, there is very little published data about infiltration rates through the walls of established homes. Our solution is to list reasonable assumptions in Table 6-4 for each of our classes of FM homes. By now you have probably decided on the class of home you occupy. Select the applicable leakage rate from Table 6-4 and calculate your wall infiltration rate on that basis. Then, after you have calculated your heat loss for the entire home (including basement losses from the basement as described in the next chapter), note whether your calculations in terms of fuel dollars are more than 20% off from your actual expenditures. If so, you may have badly estimated some or all of your infiltration losses. Reexamine your windows, doors and walls again. Perhaps you have misjudged them on the high or low side.

TABLE 6-4. WALL INFILTRATION RATES

DWELLING CLASS	LEAKAGE RATE FT³/FT² × HR
Drafty	30.0
Average	5.0
Modern	1.0
90–75	*
Superior	.5
Ultra	.1

*Not specified

You may judge walls by the following criteria:

- Poor: loose, warped lap siding; loose, warped shingles; masonry without exterior stucco or interior plaster.
- Good: Solid lap siding or shingles with fresh paint over insulating sheathing; masonry with exterior stucco or interior plaster or insulating board in the cavity wall.
- Very Good: any wall with vapor barrier consisting of solid plastic sheet; aluminum or vinyl siding over established wall.

Window frames are a troublesome source of infiltration. Once they are made there is not much you can do about them except apply caulk.

Wind has a great deal to do with infiltration in walls. The rates may be 50% less than those quoted here when the wind is mild, or 50% more when the wind is over 25 mph.

We summarize in Table 6-5 the IL losses for the FM homes, assuming that the householder has been able to achieve the standards of Table 6-4.

TABLE 6-5. INFILTRATION LOSSES OF FM WALLS, MBTU

VU		557	92.9	18.6		9.3	1.3
Td	DD	DRAFTY	AVERAGE	MODERN	90–75	SUPERIOR	ULTRA
34	1000	6.6	1.1	.22		.11	.022
47	2000	18.4	3.1	.60	Not	.31	.061
54	3000	31.7	5.3	1.10	Applicable.	.53	.110
58	4000	45.3	7.6	1.50	Leakage	.76	.150
63	5000	61.5	10.3	2.10	rate not	1.00	.200
70	6000	82.0	13.7	2.70	specified.	1.40	.270
77	7000	105.0	17.6	3.50		1.80	.350
82	8000	128.0	21.4	4.30		2.10	.430
86	9000	151.0	25.2	5.00		2.50	.500
92	10,000	179.0	30.0	6.00		3.00	.600

OPTIONS FOR WALL UPGRADING

You have only three ways to upgrade the insulation of your walls: add it to the outside, add it to the inside, or put it between the inside and outside. There are several variations on the basics.

Upgrading with In-Wall Insulation

For an illustration let us take the Average FM home and see what improvements we can achieve by putting insulation inside the walls. We assume that this home has a frame construction whose wall consists of lap siding, 1/2" insulating sheathing, no insulation and gypsum wallboard. The U value of this wall is .225, and the AU factor is 233. This type of wall can have its insulation resistance greatly increased by forcing insulation into the spaces between the studs. Vendors are anxious to sell you foam, fiberglass, mineral wool or cellulose. Foam is pumped into the space, and the others are blown in.

Foam in the wall will increase the wall resistance to 23.43, giving an AU factor of 44.46 and a seasonal XL of 6.55 MBTU in a 6000 DD climate. Note from Table 6-3 that you have by this simple step increased the class of your walls from Average to Ultra. The blown insulation is a bit less effective in this application. The total wall resistance becomes 17.25, and the AU factor becomes 59.94, giving a seasonal XL of 8.83 MBTU in a 6000 DD climate.

Foam is also very effective in reducing the infiltration losses. While no comparative data are available, our reasoned guess is that it could reduce the infiltration by about one level from those given in Table 6-4.

If your home has been built to good standards within the past twenty years, you probably have insulating sheathing and 2" of roll insulation in the walls. The foam people will tell you that you can still pump foam into these walls. The foam compresses the roll insulation, causing it to lose some of its insulating value but allowing the entrance of about 2 1/2" of foam. The AU factor of this wall then becomes about 60.97, giving you an XL of 8.98 MBTU per season in the 6000 DD climate and putting you in the Superior class. Some vendors claim that they can pump out the old insulation enabling them to fill the entire space with foam and upgrading the wall somewhat. Our computations show that you would gain about 2 MBTU, or $10 a year, by this choice. Will the extra expense for removal of the old insulation be justified by that much saving? The answer can be resolved by asking this question: Will this extra energy saving, when combined with other savings that I can introduce, enable me to move my

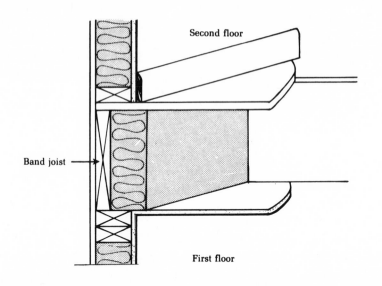

Second floor

Band joist →

First floor

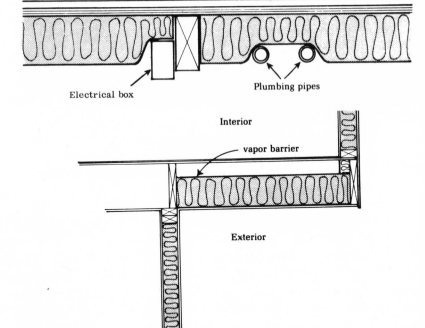

Electrical box

Plumbing pipes

Interior

vapor barrier

Exterior

Where to insulate walls and floors

home into the Superior or Ultra class? The $10 a year saving would probably not justify the extra expense, but if it enables you to accomplish your aim removing the old insulation would be a wise choice. Sometimes the economic evaluation of energy leads to a distortion of true value.

The benefits, from an economic standpoint, of putting insulation into an uninsulated wall are dramatically influenced by climate. Note in the following list the saving achieved by adding foam to an Average FM wall:

```
1000 DD—  2.26 MBTU—$  11.30
3000 DD—10.71 MBTU—$  53.56
6000 DD—27.77 MBTU—$138.85
9000 DD—51.17 MBTU—$255.85
```

Upgrading with Outside Insulation

If the outside of your home looks tacky, or if the siding is warped or rotted, or if you are fed up with the expense and work of repeated painting, you may consider refinishing with one of the permanent color sidings, such as aluminum or vinyl. If you do go the route of home improvement, you should insist that the new siding have an underlayment of at least 1″ of polystyrene board. The added insulation will reduce the AU factor by more than 1/2 for an Average home and by 1/3 for a Modern home. The Average home in a 6000 DD climate would save about 18 MBTU, or $90, per year, and the Modern home 5 MBTU, or $25.

Upgrading Interior Walls

If you have been wanting to add wood paneling, you might now plan to do so. But be sure to consider applying a 1″ or 2″ layer of polystyrene board directly to any wall facing the outdoors before adding the paneling. One inch of polystyrene will add, with the paneling, 5.31 resistance to the wall. One difficulty, of course, is that you probably want to panel only one or two rooms of your home. This improvement will not result in any exciting amount of energy conservation. Remember, however, that we are looking to save every Btu wherever possible. Therefore, the 2 MBTU you could save this way may be worth thinking about. There is one complication. Your window and door frames as presently constructed will not come level with the new wall thickness. Unless you or your carpenter have some good ideas about how to enlarge these frames, you must forget about adding insulation back of the wall paneling.

What about built-in bookcases? If you add these to an outside wall, be sure to glue a panel of polystyrene to the wall before building in the bookcases. What about remodeling your kitchen? Put insulating board to the outside wall before you put up the cabinets.

INSULATING MASONRY WALLS

If you have a cavity between the inner and outer layers of brick or block, you can have foam insulation pumped into this opening. The cavity will be about 2″ thick, and the foam will enable you to increase the R value by about 10. If you do not know whether you have a cavity wall, your foam insulation vendor will be glad to do an exploratory drilling to find out.

Sometimes the interior of a poured or block concrete wall is left unfinished, or perhaps finished with a scratch coat of plaster. You can easily add 2″ of insulating board and a finish layer of gypsum board to this wall and increase the wall resistance by R10 or better. This treatment is especially desirable on the north wall. You must use a reasoned judgement, however, about adding it to the south wall. As you will soon see, a masonry wall is very desirable for storing heat on the sunny side of the house. If you have an exposed masonry wall on the south, east or west, or as an interior wall on any side, you have a ready-made opportunity to exploit the solar gain from the south windows.

Yes, a masonry wall can be insulated on the outside. The technique is to apply 2″ of urethane foam to the outside of the masonry wall and then trowel a layer of "Blocbond" (fiberglass reinforced mortar) to the foam to give it a weather resistant finish. Solid urethane board may be used instead of the foam. This treatment permits the masonry wall to be used as a heat storage mass while minimizing the escape of heat by transmission. You would not be able to use this technique on brick walls, however, unless you were willing to lose the aesthetic value of the brick home.

UPGRADING BY LANDSCAPING

The standard average wind speed used by designers is 15 mph in winter and 7 1/2 mph in summer. If you could reduce the winter wind speeds from 15 to 7 1/2 mph, your Modern home in a 6000 DD climate would save about .14 MBTU per year. This saving is nothing to get excited about, but, if you are doing landscaping anyway, you might as well think about getting some energy benefit. Planting windbreaker evergreens on the north or northwest sides will help, although, unfortunately, there is no quantitative measure to tell us by how many mph you will reduce the windspeed.

Do not plant evergreens on the east, south or west sides of the house close enough that they will shade the house when full grown. You want the benefit of solar gain through the windows and on the walls. Some kinds of deciduous trees with open branches, such as walnut, are suitable on the south if they are planted at a distance where they will shade the house in summer but shade the house only from the top branches in winter. Avoid shrubs close to the house on the south side.

7

What To Do About Floors and Basements

WHAT TO DO ABOUT FLOORS

Most homes having a basement or crawl space have a central heating system in the basement. It is common practice to leave the furnace and heat ducts or pipes without insulating cover. The escaping heat raises the basement temperature to about that of the heated spaces above so that there is virtually no heat loss through the floor, and in some cases there may be heat gain. Insulation is seldom put in the floor over a heated basement.

If the floor is above an unheated space, the floor should be treated somewhat like a ceiling, although the numbers will be different. Instead of a layer of gypsum board or lath and plaster, the surface will probably consist of subflooring and finish flooring adding up to wood 1 1/4" to 1 1/2" thick plus, perhaps, carpeting or linoleum. The surface resistance will be higher (R .92) because that is the characteristic of a downward flow of heat.

We take .284 as the U value of the typical uncovered floor, .278 as the U value of the floor with linoleum covering and .21 as the U value if the floor is covered with carpeting with a pad.

The air at the floor level is probably 2 or 3 degrees lower than at thermostat level, especially over an unheated basement. If the unheated basement has ventilation to the outside air, the inside air is probably at the same temperature.

From these data you should be able to compute the heat loss of your floor, if you have an unheated under space, using the standard XL equation. Infiltration loss through the floor will be little if any.

If your floor is over an unheated space and it is not insulated, you could be losing over 30 MBTU per year in a typical northern winter from that source alone. This floor needs insulation badly, not only to prevent so much heat loss but also to improve personal comfort. No one can feel comfortable in a room with a cold floor. But if the space under the floor is difficult to get into or too shallow to crawl through, you have a real problem. Should you go to the trouble and expense of excavating under the house in order to be able to install insulation? At times like these you must be clever and ingenious.

One of the ingenious answers would be to shore up the foundation on the outside with plaster and insulation and Blocbond to the point where it is virtually leakproof and then to pump solar heat into the space.

The fact that you could be losing so much heat through your floor is one of the reasons why it is so depressing to contemplate most of the prevailing ideas about retrofitting solar heat to a home. Unless you really batten down the hatches at all points to keep the heat from escaping, you could spend thousands of dollars on a solar system just to circulate heat into a house and out again. There's no one to come into your home and tell you which hatches are leaking, at least not at the price you can afford. It could be done at a reasonable price, and the service will probably be offered some day, but you would still have to pay the price of adding the insulation before the solar system made sense. Under prevailing ideas this service will recommend 600 to 800 square feet of collector with a probable solar input of about 60% of your load. We are offering you ideas that will enable you to get by with 200 to 300 square feet of collector while relieving you entirely, 100%, from dependence on fossil fuel. But to achieve this state we reiterate that you must learn to be your own heating and solar engineer. We think you ought to buy the hardware, but you ought to be the one to specify it. These comments get us a little ahead of our story.

If your basement is heated by a furnace, and if you upgrade your home to the Superior class, you may need to re-evaluate the benefits of insulation under the floor. As you lose less and less heat and depend more and more on solar gain, your furnace will operate less and less, and your average basement temperature will drop. During some of the normal heating months, such as October, November, March and April, your furnace may hardly run at all. You would have to measure your basement temperature during these months and evaluate your heat loss carefully to determine whether floor insulation is worth the cost in this situation.

HEAT LOSS IN BASEMENTS

We have pointed out that, if your calculated heat loss for your entire home turns out to be way out of line with your fuel bill, you may have badly estimated your infiltration loss. If your calculation is low, you may have forgotten to include your basement losses.

Under most conditions a concrete floor in a heated basement will lose about 2 Btu per hour per square foot. Poured concrete walls 8″ thick will lose about twice as much for that portion below grade. The R value for that portion of the wall above the grade will be that of a normal concrete 8″ wall, R .64. These values are fair approximations for all climates.

We do not need to include climate factors to determine the seasonal heat loss for basement sections below grade because the ground remains a fairly constant temperature. We simply multiply the heat loss per hour per square foot by the number of hours and number of square feet. For climates below 3000 DD we arbitrarily say that the heating season runs from November through March, or 3624 hours. For climates above 3000 DD we say the heating season runs from October through April, or 5088 hours. The equation for computing the transmission heat loss through the basement floor is:

$$XL = A \times 2 \times hr$$

For that portion of the basement wall below grade use 4 Btu per hour per square foot as the loss rate for a poured concrete wall. For a concrete block wall you might use 3 Btu, and for either wall in climates above 5000 DD you might use 5 Btu as the loss rate. The equation for the below grade basement wall is:

$$XL = A \times 4 \times hr$$

The equation for the portion of the basement wall above grade is the conventional one. It is:

$$XL = AUTd \times 24 \times .95 \times DD/65$$

Table 7-1 shows the transmission heat losses of the FM homes in the various climates. Note that we do not show any calculations for the Drafty home. This class of home may have been built before the common use of the poured concrete basement floor and wall. The variations in wall structure during this era are too numerous to classify. If you have this type of basement wall, we must ask you to compute the loss using the data and procedures already described here.

TABLE 7-1. BASEMENT HEAT LOSSES OF FM HOMES, MBTU

Td	DD	DRAFTY	AVERAGE	MODERN	90–75	SUPERIOR	ULTRA
34	1000		13.9	11.1	21.0	10.1	5.3
47	2000		15.6	11.9	21.0	10.4	5.4
54	3000	Not	17.6	12.7	21.2	10.6	5.6
58	4000	Applicable.	24.9	17.6	23.8	15.0	7.8
63	5000		27.3	18.3	23.8	15.3	8.0
70	6000		30.4	19.1	21.8	15.6	8.2
77	7000		33.9	19.8	21.2	16.1	8.5
82	8000		37.3	20.4	19.8	16.5	8.7
86	9000		40.7	21.3	19.2	17.0	9.0
92	10,000		45.0	22.0	17.9	17.5	9.3

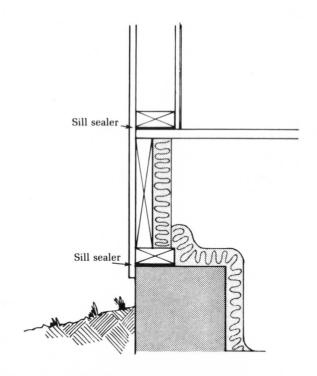

There is a small amount of infiltration loss in a basement. Where the sill rests on the foundation there is a crack, even though it may be small. The sill bears the weight of the house, so there is a press fit with the foundation. There is always a certain amount of graininess and waviness in the top of the foundation, so there always remains numerous small leakage paths. This leakage rate is probably about 10 cubic feet per hour per linear foot. The better construction places a layer of insulation between the sill and the foundation, which cuts the infiltration loss in half. Service entrances for water, gas, electricity and oil, unless well caulked, can be infiltration sources. Table 7-2 shows the probable infiltration losses of the FM homes.

TABLE 7-2. INFILTRATION LOSSES FROM FM BASEMENTS, MBTU

DD	DRAFTY, AVERAGE, MODERN	SUPERIOR, ULTRA
1000	.28	.14
2000	.77	.39
3000	1.30	.66
4000	1.90	.95
5000	2.60	1.30
6000	3.40	1.70
7000	4.40	2.20
8000	5.40	2.60
9000	6.40	3.20
10,000	7.60	3.80

HEAT LOSS FROM SLAB FLOORS

Slab floors are either unheated or heated. The unheated variety is found in homes where the heat distribution is by conventional means. In the heated variety, heat distribution is through the floor itself; the concrete is heated by hot water or hot air ducts buried in the concrete.

It has been found that for either type of slab the heat loss is almost entirely through the edges of the slab for the usual size of home. That is, the heat loss is a function of the perimeter of the house, not the square footage of the slab.

It is common practice to insulate the edges of the slab with waterproof insulating board. The insulating board may project straight down into the ground, or it may curve around the edge and go under the slab. In either case, the width of the insulating board would be about 2 feet.

The heat loss per hour is calculated from the equation,

$$XL = Btuh \times Perimeter.$$

The coefficient, Btuh, can be obtained from the curves shown in the graph on page 96. The seasonal heat loss is then determined by multiply-

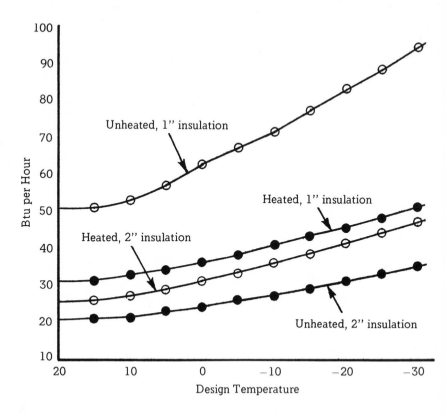

Heat Loss from Slab Floors.

ing the XL so obtained by the hours in the heating season. The equations are:

to 3000 DD, $Q = XL \times 3624 \times .2$
above 3000 DD, $Q = XL \times 5088 \times .5$

If the perimeter is without insulation, the heat loss will be about twice the loss from 1″ of insulation.

If you have edge insulation, you can upgrade it by digging down two feet and adding an additional layer. If you have one inch of edge insulation and can do the digging and installation yourself, the payback period will be 6 to 8 years. If you have no edge insulation, you should make an effort to apply at least two inches.

UPGRADING BASEMENTS

The easiest way to upgrade a basement, in most cases, is to apply insulation to the wall. You apply 1″ furring strips to the wall (drill into the concrete and put in expansion screws), fill in between the strips with polystyrene board and finish off with gypsum board or wood paneling. The FM home in a 6000 DD climate would save more than 10 MBTU by this treatment. You could, of course, increase the thickness of the insulation by increasing the thickness of the furring strips.

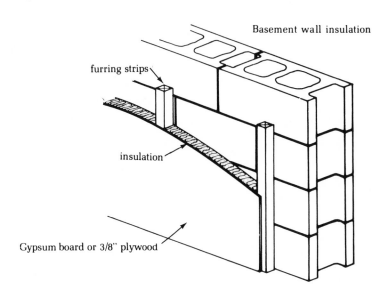

When insulation is applied to the basement walls, the workmen usually stop at the top of the wall where the floor joists rest on the concrete. This space from the top of the foundation wall to the subflooring and between the floor joists extends out to the skin of the house, which probably consists of no more than a strip of insulating board and a layer of siding. This space, some 10″ to 12″ wide and the length of the house, is the forgotten heat escape route of most homes. If you insulate the basement wall of your home, you should run the gypsum board or paneling all the way up between the floor joists to the subflooring and stuff the space back of it with loose insulation or bat insulation. In addition to blocking conduction loss, you will also reduce infiltration to an insignificant amount.

If you are striving for an Ultra class home, you may consider laying a wood floor over the concrete. Laying 2″ × 4″ joists over the concrete, filling between with R 11 insulation and finishing with 3/4″ plywood and linoleum will increase the resistance of your basement floor by R 12.02. The Ultra home of Table 7-1 has this treatment.

If you have been thinking about a rumpus room in the basement, you should add it in a way to enhance the energy efficiency of your home. For example, if you do not intend to finish off the entire basement, try to have two sides of the rumpus room against the exterior wall. Use 2″ × 4″ studding for these sides and fill the space between with urea foam; finish as you desire with gypsum board or decorative plywood. Consider the possibility of leaving the ceiling in this room unfinished. Remember that it is undesirable to have any portion of the main floor unheated if you have a heated basement; to do so will cause cold spots and uneven control of temperature in the main portion of the house.

The family room, so popular for the past two decades, may often be an unrecognized source of much transmission loss. These rooms are usually on the lower floor of a tri-level or split level and almost always have a concrete slab on the ground. These concrete floors are more like basement floors than slab floors, however. In a true unheated slab floor the heat loss is almost entirely through the edges. It has been designed so that the slab and the ground underneath act like a heat storage, and the floor is therefore usually about as warm as the house. The floor in the family room is not designed this way. It usually feels cold to the feet. Since it acts like a basement, it loses heat at the rate of about 2 Btu per hour per square foot. You might give serious consideration to laying insulation and a wood floor over the concrete floor of the family room.

WET BASEMENTS

If you have water problems in the basement, it will not be easy for you to upgrade the energy efficiency of your basement. Remember that wet insulation is worse than no insulation because water conducts heat better than air. If water accumulates in the basement, an insulated wooden floor is probably out because sump pumps are notoriously undependable. Use of gypsum board and similar materials is out. Fortunately, there are waterproof insulations, such as those used to insulate the edges of slabs, and this type should be used if there is any indication that water might ever be a problem.

8

What To Do
About
Add-On Rooms

When the home is too small for your needs you can either move to a larger home or add a room. For adding rooms we do not describe procedures and methods and designs. Rather, we summarize the considerations you should keep in mind in order to achieve energy efficiency—even to increase the energy efficiency of your total home.

HEAT LOSS

Adding a room gives you the opportunity to build the way the designer of an Ultra home would build. Here are some of the things you would do:

- Increase the wall insulation. Use 2″ × 6″ studs instead of the common 2″ × 4″ size. Place the studs on 24″ centers instead of the common 16″ spacing. The extra cost of studs will be compensated by the fewer number required. Use foil-backed gypsum board for the interior finish. Use 3/4″ insulating sheathing on the exterior finish. Fill the space between studs with urea foam insulation. For a vapor barrier use a plastic film tacked to the studs before adding the gypsum board. You will now have achieved a wall with a U value of about .03. During the very coldest nights of the winter the walls of your added room will be losing heat at the rate of about 2 Btuh while the rest of your home will be losing it at the rate of 7 to 20 Btuh.
- Make sure that there is at least an insulating value of R 38 between your ceiling and the outside. Depending on the details of your construction, ensure that there is adequate attic ventilation according to the principles outlined in Chapter 3.
- Try to avoid putting in north windows, if possible. If they must be included, use the smallest practical size and use triple pane glazing.
- If you include a fireplace, remember that the ordinary fireplace wastes more heat than it supplies. It consumes the air in the room you have gone to the expense to heat. Then, it causes lowered pressure in the house, thus sucking in a lot more cold air through the infiltration routes. Then, when the fireplace is not burning, the air in the house rushes up the chimney, if you forget to close the damper. When building new construction, be sure to

include a duct from the outside air to the fireplace combustion chamber, and make sure that the duct has a tight damper. Consider the possibility of using a tight-fitting glass front plate over the fireplace to reduce these air losses both during and after operation.

□ If you include an outside door, make sure that the prime door is 2" solid hardwood. Supply a quality-type storm door. If this door is to be a main entrance, try to work out a design that will include a vestibule or other type of enclosure.

□ If you use a slab floor for the new room, be sure to put in edge insulation on the perimeter of the slab. Use waterproof insulation 2" thick and 2' wide, and curve the insulation so that it projects under the slab. That is, the insulation should be put in place before the cement is poured. If you build on a foundation, such as concrete blocks two or three layers high, put R30 bat or roll insulation between the floor joists. Be sure to put two small windows in this foundation for cross ventilation to prevent moisture condensation in the insulation.

HEAT GAIN

Try to make the added room supply more heat than it uses so that its surplus can be distributed to the rest of the house and thus contribute to the energy efficiency of the home. Consider the following ideas when making your plans:

□ Think about designing a solar window into the south wall of the room according to the principles discussed in Chapter 9. Since the amount of solar heat gain will depend on the size of the window, the amount of heat you hope to capture will influence your thinking about the size and shape of the room.

□ Consider the possibility of putting a wood stove into the room. A wood stove will supply 30,000 or more Btuh, which is 10 times what you will need to maintain comfort in this room, if you build it to Ultra class specifications. The combination of wood stove and solar window could easily contribute 300,000 Btu per day to the home heating budget. This amount is more than most homes need.

□ If you add a fireplace, make sure it is the kind that circulates the heat developed into the room. Consider the possibility of placing the fireplace on the interior wall adjoining the main house instead of on the customary exterior wall. In this way, the heat that escapes by conduction through the bricks or stone is retained inside the building.

HEAT DISTRIBUTION

If you design so that the new room produces more heat than it needs, you must also plan to distribute the surplus to other parts of the home. Here is another situation where your ingenuity must come into play. It is also another example of the kind of problem that can best be handled by self-engineering. We can offer some suggestions.

If we are to distribute heat out of this room we must think of the room as a heat source. But a heat source, to be very effective, needs to be quite a bit higher in temperature than the air it heats. That is, we are proposing to heat a space from a source that is not much warmer than the space. Our heat source room should not be above 75 for comfort, and the space to be heated should not be below 70. So we are talking about a 5 degree differential. Our "Td" is 5 degrees. It is true that we can heat an air space with a small Td, but we need a large volume air flow to do it. The smaller the Td, the larger the volume. Let us see what we can figure out about the situation.

First, how much heat does our new room require? If we have built to Ultra class standards, the average transmission coefficient of the whole envelope will be about R30, or U .033. If the room is 15 × 20 feet, it will have a heat loss rate of about 1500 Btuh on a typical day in January. If we have built a 90 square foot solar window into the south wall, and if we assume that the window can collect about 500 Btu per square foot per day on a sunny day in January, the total energy collected for the day is 45,000 Btu. In an 8 hour day the average is 5625 Btu per hour. Therefore, the surplus from the solar window over the room requirements is about 4000 Btu per hour. We have 4000 Btu per hour available for distribution at 75 degrees.

If the main section of the home has an average U value of .20 per square foot of envelope, a home of 1000 square feet of floor space will require about 30,000 Btuh on this typical January day, or 30 Btuh per square foot of floor space. If the solar window produces a surplus of 4000 Btuh, it could supply heat to 133 square feet of floor space. That is, the surplus from the new room could maintain comfort in another room having a dimension of 10 × 13.

The volume of air, V, in cubic feet per minute, that a distribution system can handle is given by the empirical equation

$$V = Btuh/1.08 \times Td$$

Then, with 4000 Btuh to distribute and Td 5,

$$V = 4000/1.08 \times 5 = 741 \text{ cfm.}$$

This equation yields the number of cubic feet per minute of air that must be moved to distribute the indicated Btuh. To move enough air to distribute 4000 Btuh you need a fan capable of moving 741 cubic feet a minute. This computation enables you to buy the right fan.

This fan should be placed in the wall in the upper part of the new room. Preferably, it should blow the heat directly into the next room instead of forcing it through a duct into rooms farther away. Instead of a wall fan it would be possible to place a large floor fan in the doorway so as to blow cool air from the main house into the solar room. This solution is inefficient, inconvenient and provides less comfort. A nice alternative would be to make a very wide opening between the new room and the main house so as, in effect, to create one large new room.

If you placed a wood stove in the new room, it would supply most of the heat required by a 1000 square foot home. It would not keep all parts of the home at a uniform comfortable temperature, however, unless the heat were ducted to the various rooms. In other words, the stove would have to act like a forced hot air furnace. This idea is within the realm of possibility. If you have been seriously thinking about going to a wood stove, one of your problems may have been, "Where shall I put it?" In these days houses are not equipped with chimneys suitable for stoves.

If you do choose to go this route, you will run into more problems than we can cover with advice here. We suggest that you talk with your local heating engineer before committing yourself too deeply.

An air duct distribution system for the added room would probably use registers near the ceiling. If you have lowered the ceiling as one home improvement, or plan to lower it, the space between the dropped ceiling and the original would be a nice place to run the duct from your new room wood furnace.

ASPECT RATIO

The most efficient shape, from a heat loss standpoint, is a sphere, because the ratio of skin to interior volume is the least of all forms. A square configuration is the closest approach to a sphere that is practical to live in.

When planning the addition of a room, can you do something to change the aspect ratio of your home to more nearly that of a square? If your home is in an L or T shape, your best solution would be to fill in one of the indentations, preferably the one with the south view if available in order to get some solar gain. If your home is rectangular, could you add the room the entire length of one side? For example, if your home is, like the FM home, 25 by 40 feet, could you add a room about 10 feet wide along the entire 40-foot side?

Some people have cut off the roof of their single story home, raised it up and built a second story, thus effectively doubling their floor space. From an energy standpoint this idea is good, if you include superior insulation during the remodeling.

Under special conditions a long, narrow home facing south is better for solar heat than a square one because you have the opportunity to install more solar window space. If your house faces south and if you wish to exploit passive solar heat, adding a long room so as to increase the south aspect is a possibility.

DORMERS

Adding dormers into the attic roof is one of the popular ways of adding rooms, but it is one of the least attractive for energy efficiency. You can improve the efficiency of your dormer when you build it by following these suggestions:

Insist that the builder use 12″ rafters for the roof and put in 8″ of roll insulation between the rafters. Specify that a vapor barrier shall be provided. Specify that the 4″ air space above the insulation be ventilated in some way, either by opening into a ventilated attic or by venting to the outside. Specify foil-backed gypsum board for the ceiling. The roof of your dormer should now be over R30.

Specify 2″ × 6″ wall studs for the sidewalls. Use R19 insulation and a vapor barrier. Use foil-backed gypsum board for the interior finish. Specify 3/4″ insulating sheathing plus 1″ of polystyrene board plus whatever exterior finish you desire. Your wall will have an R value of over 25.

Do you have a choice as to whether the dormer should face south or north? If so, choose the south orientation.

If the dormer must face north, northwest or northeast, can you tolerate no windows in any of these directions? If not, try to settle for very small windows with triple pane glass. Use regular size windows with double or triple pane glass in the east or west. If the dormer faces south, southeast or southwest, fill as much of the front as possible with double pane glass, and provide insulating shutters to block out the heat loss at night.

The usual way to prevent overheating from a large south window in the summer is to build a roof with a large overhang so as to shade the windows. A large overhang may not be practical in many dormers. You may have to plan to use insulating shutters or drapes in summer during the day as well as at night during the winter.

Assume that your dormer, built to these specifications, measures 15 × 15 feet and that you have put in 60 square feet of solar window with moveable insulation. Your seasonal heat loss in a 6000 DD climate will be about 5.8 MBTU, and your seasonal heat gain will be about 4.4 MBTU. During October and November there will be more heat gain than heat loss. If you did not use the moveable insulation, your heat loss would be about a million Btu higher.

9

Adding
Solar Heat

THE UPGRADING PAYOFF

Now we begin to reach the point of the whole essay. In Table 9-1 we summarize all of the various FM homes according to degree day climates. Pick out a line close to your own climate and follow the story across the table for the various classes of homes. This story becomes especially significant if we convert MBTU to dollars. For example, consider the MBTU in the line for the 6000 DD climate. Multiplying these numbers by $5, our standard of cost per million Btu for fuel, we get the following cost per year for heat:

- Drafty FM home: $1740
- Average FM home: $845 (51%)
- Modern FM home: $515 (39%)
- 90–75 FM home: $425
- Superior FM home: $280 (45%)
- Ultra FM home: $125 (55%)

The percentages shown are the degrees of betterment you can achieve by going up one grade. Note that in most cases (the 90–75 home is a special class) you can improve your lot better than 40% by upgrading one step.

Computing your own saving and comparing it with Table 9-1, you are able to judge how much you can afford to spend for upgrading. For example, if you wish to move an FM Average home to a Modern home in a 6000 DD climate, you will save $330 a year in fuel bills. If you wish to amortize the cost over 10 years, you may spend $3300 for the improvement.

This kind of financial reality is what limits us from doing what we ought to do. In order to do the upgrading we have to go to the bank for a home improvement loan, and the bank will talk to us in terms of 5 to 10 year repayment. The upgrading you do will last for at least 20 years and probably for the life of the house, which could be 100 years. The

TABLE 9-1.   TOTAL SEASONAL HEAT LOSSES FOR FM HOMES, MBTU

DD	DRAFTY	AVERAGE	MODERN	90–75	SUPERIOR	ULTRA
1000	40	24	18	27	14	7
2000	87	47	31	37	20	10
3000	141	71	45	48	27	13
4000	200	102	64	61	37	17
5000	266	132	81	73	45	21
6000	348	169	103	85	56	25
7000	442	212	127	98	68	30
8000	534	254	152	110	79	35
9000	627	297	176	120	90	40
10,000	772	405	206	133	106	46

economic facts of life tell us how much per month we can pay on a loan. If we can pay only the amount we save on fuel bills, then our upgrading has to have that limit.

Very often the upgrading we have been talking about for fuel economy is the kind of home improvement you want to do anyway. In this case, the fuel saving is an add-on value. The fuel saving should not be used as the sole criterion for judging the amount you can spend.

Table 9-1 shows us some important data to consider, if we think about adding solar heat. It shows that as the conservation class goes up the need for heat goes down. And the amount of solar heat we need to add goes down.

You may have already investigated the possibility of adding solar collectors as a way to cut down on your fuel bill. Consider the implications. An "active" solar heating system will produce about 94,000 Btu per heating season per square foot of collector (reference, *The Buy Wise Guide to Solar Heat,* Floyd Hickok, St. Petersburg, Fla.: Hour House, 1976). A Modern home in a 6000 DD climate would require over 1000 square feet of collector to supply 100% of the heat. At $15 a square foot from the solar system, this "home improvement" would cost $15,000. This price tag is out of the question for most people. Furthermore, 1000 square feet of collector would not supply 100% of the need during December, January and February unless you have a very large storage tank, and then the price goes to a lot more than $15 a square foot. The answer is supposed to be to use solar as a supplement to standard heat, expecting it to supply 50% to 60% of the requirement. In this case, a system with about 500 square feet of collector would be required. Usually collectors are roof-mounted. Our FM home has only about 600 square feet of roof.

St. Louis, Missouri

Two Typical Solar Homes

Atlanta, Georgia

We shall demonstrate in this chapter that the concept of the active solar heating system as a *supplement* to conventional fuel is the wrong way to go. Or, rather we shall demonstrate that the concept of integrating an active solar system with total energy management is a better way to go. At the heart of this concept is the idea that the less heat you lose the less solar input you need, and, if you can get the heat loss low enough, your solar input can be small and not very capital intensive. In this case, your back-up heat is the supplement, and, since the need is small, the back-up system can be small and inexpensive.

You can see now why we have developed the gradation diagram of Table 9-1. The heart of the solar idea is conservation. If we can get conservation upgraded high enough, the amount of solar attachment becomes so small as to be within the realm of practical cost. The rule is: *Don't buy solar until you have got your heat loss down.*

In one case, we figured that an Ultra home in a 6000 DD climate required only 1/3 cord of wood during a heating season as supplemental fuel.

SOLAR HEAT

Most of the information you can get on solar space heating assumes that you are building a custom-designed home incorporating the solar energy feature, much as you might include a built-in appliance. This attitude was common back in the days, about 50 years ago, when the concept of central heat began to appear as a desirable built-in feature. After that concept began to take hold, it soon became so common that no one would think of building without central heat. Much the same attitude prevails today about solar space heat. Many solar advocates seem to think that solar will make the same kind of transition. We suggest that there are different forces at work.

If you are already established in your own home and have no intention of building, what are you to believe? Are you going to be able to add solar in the same way folks used to add central heat to an old home? Or, in the way you buy a dishwasher? We think not. You belong to that vast army known as the "retrofit market," and the problems of retrofit are unique. If you are truly interested in solar space heat, what can you do about it?

If you were building a new, custom-designed home, you would learn a lot about the technology of solar energy, and you would learn a lot about the cost. You would learn that it is going to cost from $15 to $25 per square foot of collector for the system. The designer would talk to you about payback period assuming certain rates of interest in cost of fossil fuel and certain interest rates. You would hear a great deal about the per cent of back-up heat needed. It is supposed to be good design if you can get solar to provide 50% to 60% of your needs and only have to call on conventional fuels for 40% to 50%.

Much of this kind of talk is irrelevant to those designers who have been able to switch their thinking from the notion of solar as a supplement to the concept of the true solar house—the Ultra Solar Home.

There are four steps to the design of an Ultra Solar Home:

☐ Insulate and conserve heat to the maximum
☐ Increase the amount of passive solar heat
☐ Add sufficient active solar input to provide 100% solar heat for all but the two or three worst months
☐ Provide a simple back-up system to make up the difference between demand and solar input during these few worst months.

At first the idea of the Ultra Solar Home sounds much like the way we used to think about adding central heat. Actually, the two concepts are in different worlds. The Ultra Solar Home reduces the demand for heat so much that a relatively small active solar collector will supply all the needs except during the worst months, and the need for extra heat during these months is so small that it can be supplied by inexpensive means. A very small conventional heat source without expensive piping or ducting, a wood stove, or a heat-distributing fireplace are often enough to supply all the supplemental heat needed. The small amount of active system plus the small back-up system can end up costing only a little more than a conventional heating system.

This mode of thinking directs the design of a new Ultra Solar Home. What about retrofit design? The main difference is that you probably have the back-up system already in operation. You probably already have a central heating system. There is nothing to prevent you from upgrading the conservation of your home to the Ultra class, adding passive solar gain, and adding enough solar collection to supply all your needs for 9 months of the year. Your back-up system is way over designed for your new needs. It simply operates less and less frequently as you get closer and closer to the Ultra home ideal. We realize that the heating engineers say that this way of running a furnace is inefficient operation, but we can surely tolerate inefficiency to that extent in exchange for not having to buy a new back-up system. You will, no doubt, put your active solar output into the furnace distribution system and thus save a big expense in the solar installation.

We maintain that you can apply the four basic rules to retrofit as well as you can to new construction. The first hurdle is to upgrade your conservation to at least the Superior class. The other steps then are easy. You can hear plenty of whiners complain that "someday maybe" solar will become practical if "they" can get the price down, or if they can make it work. The whiners assume that we must depend on our old, tried-and-true redeemers, mass production and technological improvement, to accomplish these two keys to accepting solar heat the way we accepted central furnaces. The plain fact is price is no barrier in the Ultra Solar Home concept. As for technology, solar collectors are about as efficient now as they are ever going to be regardless of how sophisticated they become; if they fail to work the fault is with systems engineering and installation, not with the collector (assuming a quality manufactured collector).

The four basic rules apply as well to an established home as to new construction. The only difference is that for established construction you do not have as many opportunities to apply little tricks that save a few Btu's here and there. But, as long as you know what you are doing and where you want to go, there is no reason you cannot work at the four rules in your established home just as effectively as though you were building a new home.

We have shown how you can move from whatever class you are in to a better class by upgrading the various causes of heat loss. By diligent and thoughtful upgrading you can gradually move from your present state to a better and better class. It is entirely within practical possibility for most homes to move to the Superior class, if not the Ultra class.

We do not say that you must move to the Superior or Ultra class at once. Let it be a several year goal, if you wish. This upgrading is in the nature of home improvements. As will all home improvements, you cannot do all of the things you want to do at once. You have to spread them out as best you can.

The big rule for everyone in the retrofit market is: Do not spend any money on home improvements unless you can see how the improvement can be made to upgrade your home toward a better class of energy efficiency. We add this recommendation: Do not spend money on an active solar system until you have moved your home to at least the Superior class of energy efficiency, and preferably to the Ultra class.

MONTHLY CALCULATIONS

Before you start figuring out the requirements for adding solar heat to your home, you must acquire data about energy on a monthly basis.

For your heat loss calculations we asked that you obtain the annual degree day rating of your locality from your oil dealer, your newspaper weatherman, or from your local Weather Bureau. Remember that for our FM home calculations we assumed, in most cases, that the seasonal DD from October through April is the same as the annual DD. In southern and northern climates, this assumption is not true; it was simply a convenient way for us to deal with the calculations. If you wished to get a more accurate comparison of your own case with the FM homes, you could use the 7-month DD data for your locality instead of the annual data usually quoted. However, the difference between annual and seasonal data, except perhaps for climates below 2000 DD and above 8000 DD, is not likely to be so great as to throw off the validity of your comparison.

We suggested that when you obtain the annual DD information for your locality you obtain it on the monthly basis, too. If you do not have it, now is the time to acquire it. You will be using it in this Chapter.

You also need to know the amount of solar energy available per month in your area. We summarize the data in Table 9-2. These numbers are close approximation. They are not accurate enough for a designer, but, since you probably have no way to obtain actual measurements, these numbers are close enough for your practical needs. The numbers in the table represent the amount of solar energy, in millions of Btu per month, falling on one square foot of collector surface. Note that the numbers are listed for both a vertical surface and a slanted surface; the slope of the slanted surface is 15 degrees greater than the reference latitude, which is the recommended angle for best collection of winter solar energy. You will need to make use of both of these numbers in your calculations. If you do not live on the reference latitude, interpolate between adjacent numbers to get your own value.

TABLE 9-2. MONTHLY CLEAR DAY INSOLATION PER SQUARE FOOT, MBTU

MONTH	ANGLE	LATITUDE, DEGREES			
		32	40	48	56
Oct.	Vertical	.0455	.0473	.0470	.0435
	Slanted	.0663	.0621	.0565	.0483
Nov.	Vertical	.0490	.0484	.0432	.0390
	Slanted	.0623	.0564	.0475	.0348
Dec.	Vertical	.0532	.0500	.0414	.0262
	Slanted	.0625	.0550	.0433	.0266
Jan.	Vertical	.0529	.0510	.0436	.0310
	Slanted	.0642	.0575	.0466	.0313
Feb.	Vertical	.0462	.0475	.0453	.0393
	Slanted	.0632	.0585	.0519	.0424
Mar.	Vertical	.0398	.0450	.0482	.0630
	Slanted	.0685	.0660	.0620	.0567
Apr.	Vertical	.0390	.0333	.0394	.0380
	Slanted	.0623	.0610	.0587	.0562
TOTAL	Vertical	.3226	.3225	.3081	.2600
	Slanted	.4493	.4165	.3665	.2963

PASSIVE HEAT GAIN

So far in this book we have talked about how to upgrade your home by increasing its heat conservation capacity. Note that the classes of homes we derived are characterized by diminishing amounts of heat loss, achieved primarily by increasing the insulation and reducing the infiltration. Each class of home is based on increasingly effective means of preventing the natural escape of heat. Now we want to discuss the ways to increase the natural gain of heat into the home.

When we discussed ways to reduce heat loss from windows, we noted that there is a significant amount of heat gain through windows and that the effective heat loss was obtained by subtracting the heat gain from the calculated heat loss. Now we want to notice how to augment the amount of heat gain.

The usual way to augment heat gain by ''natural,'' or ''passive,'' means is to increase the area of the south window. There is heat gain on the south wall, too, but we have blocked almost all of it from entering the house by means of insulation. The only way solar energy can get through opaque walls is by conduction. The way most of it gets through windows is by transmission of light through glass. Augmentation of heat gain can therefore be achieved by increasing the amount of light transmitted into the house, which means increasing the area of the windows.

PASSIVE SOLAR HEAT

Any building is a collector of solar energy. When a designer uses sophisticated engineering techniques to enhance and control this natural input, he says he has designed a passive solar system. This term contrasts with the "active" system, which accumulates heat in a separate, specialized solar collector and distributes the heat to the building by some sort of forced mechanical system. Active systems distribute heat at a somewhat higher temperature than do passive systems.

Passive system designers strive to use the least possible amount of mechanical transport. The purists among passive system designers spurn all mechanical distribution of heat, partly from false pride, and partly on the logical basis that, if you are going to expend some energy, you should rationally use it directly in the form of heat rather than as mechanical input.

Passive systems can supply a very large percentage of the yearly heat requirements. However, unless there is rather skillful engineering design, the occupants must either put up with quite wide swings of inside temperature or be prepared to control the interior heat by auxiliary input and by ventilation. Much of the research being carried out on the passive system relates to the application of storage in a way to smooth out the wide fluctuations of the simple passive system. There are two ways to smooth out the fluctuations: the brute force method of using a large amount of storage mass, or the decoupling method of partially separating the storage from the room.

Passive designs usually concentrate on using the south wall of the building for solar input, either as a solar window, or as an opaque solar collector. We shall note some ideas on how you might remodel your home so as to retrofit it for passive solar heat.

PASSIVE STORAGE IDEAS

Passive systems tend to build up uncomfortably high temperatures in the afternoon. The accumulated heat either has to be dumped outside or stored.

One way to store the surplus heat is by means of masonry walls. If the room receiving the solar heat has large masonry walls, they will be able to absorb the excess heat in the afternoon and then release it in the evening. The effectiveness of the concrete wall as storage will be enhanced by the application of at least 2″ of urethane on the outside protected by a coating of Blocbond. If the bare interior of the masonry is of a dark color and is kept free of drapes and pictures, it will more effectively absorb heat. If your masonry home has a single wythe of face brick or concrete block followed by an interior finish of insulation and wallboard, we do not recommend removing the insulation and wallboard just to gain access to the masonry for storage.

You would not deliberately set out to add masonry walls to your home just to store heat, except in the case where you are adding a room. If you plan for your added room to be solar heated, as we have recommended, you should consider masonry wall construction, leaving the interior unfinished.

Storage walls should have a storage capacity of 30 Btu per degree per square foot of south glass (assuming a solar window to be the solar input). This capacity is equivalent to 150 pounds of concrete. The thicker the masonry wall the more even will be the interior temperature. A wall one foot thick will maintain a temperature swing through 5 degrees, whereas a 6″ wall will have a much wider swing. The annual heat storage for either wall will be about the same, but the comfort level will be less satisfactory with a thinner wall.

If your home has a slab floor, about 5 feet of it adjacent to the solar window can be used for storage, provided you remove rugs and furniture. These floors are better than east or west walls because storage is more effective if the sun can strike masonry directly.

The ideas for storage just discussed are examples of the direct or brute force method of storing heat. We might think of the people living inside a box that serves as both a collector and storage. In the active system, the people live outside the collector box and outside the storage. In the decoupled method of passive storage, the people live inside the collector box and outside the storage medium.

The decoupled method of storage almost certainly requires mechanical transport of the heated air. As soon as we introduce mechanical transport, passive designers begin to feel they are being betrayed. However, it is the only way to maintain comfort, in many cases, and it is the practical way to keep from wasting the surplus collected by the solar window.

We examined an example of decoupled storage in the last chapter when we discussed blowing the surplus from the added room into the adjacent room. Sometimes this treatment is all that is required to dispose of the surplus and maintain comfort in the solar room.

In the best cases, however, the solar input is far in excess of what can be handled by direct storage and by distribution to adjacent rooms. Unless that amount is delivered by the solar window, it will not contribute enough to the energy budget to achieve the reduction in active input we are seeking. There should be enough passive solar input to heat the entire home in the evening and even into the next day when the sun does not shine.

One way to decouple storage from the passive source is to blow the warm air from the top of the solar room into a storage container, such as a bin of rocks located in the basement or other convenient place. By a damper control system the heat is then blown out of the rocks into the room when needed.

SOLAR WINDOWS

When you start thinking about remodeling your home for a solar window, you must survey your home for certain conditions. You must have a large expanse of south wall. The orientation should be at least within 10 degrees of true south. There must be little or no obstruction from trees during the winter months. The interior of the house should permit a large expanse of window. Preferably, the window should look into a large living room. Kitchens are not very good for conversion of light to heat; the cook likes a cool kitchen. Bedrooms are not very good either because they should be cooler than the rest of the home. In order to attain a good solar room on the south side you might even have to modify the interior layout of the house.

You must watch your pennies if you plan to install a solar window. Your aim is to pay the least possible amount for each solar Btu collected. Some claim that passive systems deliver solar energy more cheaply than active systems; the claim is not necessarily true. By doing a few calculations from Table 9-2, you can see that a vertical solar window is exposed to from 13% to 39% less insolation during a season than an active collector slanted to the optimum angle. A solar window should cost no more than half that of an active collector, if its cost per delivered Btu is to be less. If $15 a square foot is a normal price for an active collector system, then the solar window should not cost more than about $7 a square foot.

Unless you watch your quotations carefully and shop wisely, you will find that a solar window will be expensive. Consider that a picture window, which is several times smaller than the one you are seeking, costs over $12 a square foot, and sealed, double pane insulating glass costs $10 a square foot. If your carpenter wants to charge you $5 a square foot for doing your remodeling job and installing the window, then you can only afford $2 a square foot for the glass. You are at a disadvantage compared to the person who is including a solar window in a new construction. He is able to charge a lot of his cost to wall cost because he has to have a wall anyway. Your solar window has to bear all the cost of ripping out and rebuilding because you already have a wall and don't have to rebuild it.

You would be wise to seek a vendor who specializes in glass and work closely with him. You will be putting in pieces of glass 6 or 7 feet high and 4 to 6 feet wide. Ordinary window glass will not do. It must be capable of withstanding high wind pressure without breaking. You would like to have low iron glass for maximum solar transmission, but you may not be able to specify that grade. You might be able to pick up some bargains from the specialist vendor. Sometimes he has surplus pieces of sealed, double insulating glass that were measured wrong, and these can sometimes be had at great reductions. A word of caution about such glass is in order. Special glass of this sort is often of the heat absorbing or tinted type. For the solar window application, only the clearest glass is acceptable.

You will not find it practical to buy manufactured windows for this purpose. They are too expensive, they are not large enough, and, if you did put several of them together to get enough size, the frames would take up too much space. For the large sheets you will use the framing must be custom designed. You would be wise to work with a tradesman who has had some experience installing glass in office buildings.

Your solar window must have some kind of insulating shutter or moveable insulation or it will lose as much heat as it gains. The custom designed window offers an interesting possibility. If you separate the two panes of glass by 8 to 12 inches, you will have room for a pleated shutter between them. This shutter consists of a series of interleaved insulating boards fastened in accordion folds. They must be lowered and raised with a rope in the fashion of venetian blinds. This kind of insulating shutter is unavailable commercially at this writing. You will have to "invent" it yourself. In fact, the solar industry is so young you may have to apply your inventive genius to solve many of your problems. This possibility is not much different from what we have been telling you: if you want to get away from your fuel bills through the use of solar energy, you must learn to do some of your own engineering.

You will also need to plan for some type of traverse rod and drapes across your solar window because there will be times when you will want to restrict the amount of sunlight entering the room.

SOLAR WINDOW GAIN

You can readily calculate the approximate gain from your south windows for the entire heating season by reference to Table 4-1. However, remember our proposition: The Ultra home, and perhaps the Superior home, can be supplied 100% with solar for all months except December, January and February. We must know how much passive input we have in November and March to know how much active collector is needed to make up the difference. To obtain the monthly input from a solar window, use the data in Table 9-2 for vertical windows, and process it in the same way we developed Table 4-1.

This process consists of applying a series of derating factors to the solar input. First, reduce the solar irradiation by .60 because the sun shines only part of the time. Then, estimate the amount of diffuse radiation. For your convenience here, consider it as 20% of the solar irradiation. Now add the direct derated component and the diffuse component to obtain the average solar energy available at the outside surface of the glass. This amount is reduced to .86 going through a pane of glass and then to .60 by the conversion efficiency of the room. If there are two panes of glass, you must reduce the last amount again to .86. The whole equation is:

$$(Btu \times .60) + (Btu \times .20) \times .86 \times .60 \times .86$$
$$= Btu\text{'s per square foot available}$$
$$\text{at outside surface of double window.}$$

ALTERNATIVES TO THE SOLAR WINDOW

The solar window is a fine way to get solar heat into a home, but there are a number of objectives. There is a loss of privacy if you are too close to your neighbors, and on bright, sunny days there is too much glare in the room. There is too much heat loss at night unless you provide good moveable insulation. There is a wide and uncomfortable swing in temperature unless you successfully find ways to store and distribute the heat. Some who theorize about saving energy when using fossil fuel say you should limit the glass area to not more than 8% of the wall space. Since we recommend that you turn your sights away from dependence on conventional fuels, we must continue to favor large south windows.

There are, however, alternatives to the large south windows enabling you to use a lesser amount, or even a conventional amount, of window opening.

One of these alternatives is called the "Trombe-Michel wall." This device is a vertical concrete wall on the south side of a house covered with a piece of glass, Kalwall or plastic. The facing is held 3 or 4 inches from the wall by studding. The surface of the concrete is painted black. When the sun shines on the black concrete, the greenhouse effect induced by the facing causes the concrete to become very warm. At the bottom and top of this wall there are openings about 8" in diameter and a couple of feet apart leading from the collector space to the interior of the house. Heat circulates between the room and the collector space by convection.

The Trombe wall acts as both a collector and a storage. Some of the heat circulates into the room by convection, and the rest of it passes into the wall by conduction. After some length of time it reaches the interior side of the wall and adds heat to the room by conduction. In order to prevent heat loss at night, Beadwall is blown into the collector space. The stored heat continues to supply heat to the room by conduction for some time.

The Trombe wall is most suited to new construction. If you have a masonry home with unfinished interior and a south wall, you might consider converting it to a Trombe wall. For a masonry home this approach would be more practical than creating a solar window.

You could build a Trombe wall against the south wall of a frame house, but you would lose the benefit of storage, since the back of the wall would not be able to release its stored heat into the room. But again you could apply your ingenuity. Cover the wall with a double, instead of a single, facing, making the inner warm air collector space about 2" wide and the space between the two facing panes about 2" wide. Then add Beadwall moveable insulation to the outward space. When the insulation fills the outward space at night the inward space can continue to deliver its stored heat.

Another alternative to the solar window is the Buckley thermic diode panel, which is just coming on the market. This panel is a passive system combining both collection and storage.

The Buckley panel has two layers separated by an insulator, and both layers are filled with water. The front layer is an aluminum plate backed by a sheet of plastic. The plastic expands if the water freezes. The aluminum plate may be painted any dark color to suit the taste. The back layer is a water chamber that is connected, top and bottom, with the front section by means of connecting pipes. The heart of the Buckley panel is the thermic diode check valve in the top pipes between the two sections. When the sun heats the water in the collector to a higher temperature than the water in storage, a bouyancy-derived pressure opens the check valve, and heated water flows by convection and the thermosiphon effect into the storage layer. When the sun is not shining, the same kind of pressure has a reverse effect and causes the check valve to close, preventing further convection between the two sections and eliminating loss of heat from the stored layer. Heat is taken from the panel by causing air to circulate past the storage water.

The Buckley panel can be roof-mounted if the slope is greater than 30 degrees from horizontal. However, since the panel weighs about 700 pounds filled, it is not suitable for retrofit on the roof of most homes. For retrofit it is more suitably attached to a south wall, supporting the weight by means of a concrete ground foundation.

Steve Baer of Zomeworks built a house whose entire south wall consists of black 55 gallon steel drums filled with water. The sun warms the water, the heat is held in storage, and it is gradually released from the opposite side of the drums into the house.

Kalwall Corporation has modified the Baer idea in a project they call the "solar battery." Essentially, their project consists of a "hot box" whose south side is made of Kalwall double fiberglass panel. Inside the hot box there is a group of fiberglass tubes either 12″ or 18″ in diameter filled with water. Between the outside panel and the tubes there is a specially designed insulating curtain that can be rolled up during the day and lowered at night.

Solar energy enters through the south panel, and heat is stored in the water in the tubes. The hot box is attached to the south wall of a building, and ports at the top and bottom conduct heat into the building. Motor-driven fans circulate heat into the building as needed.

The hot box could easily be built into the south wall of new construction. For retrofit, there are many places where a hot box could be added to the side of a home without destroying the lines of the home.

The company claims that the 12″ tubes can convert and store 392 Btu, and the 18″ tube 735 Btu, per degree per running foot.

Kalwall has also developed a device, which they call the "Solar-Kal

Airheater,'' that has potential for retrofit. It is essentially an air-type solar collector fitted with a Kalwall fiberglass cover and designed to couple into a rockbin storage in the basement. The collectors can be built into or attached to the south wall, forming an interesting facade to the home, or they can be mounted on the roof. This device is not a passive system because it operates like an active system, but it is one of the collectors that can be applied to a vertical wall to take the place of a solar window.

In fact, any collector can be attached to a south wall. The main reason for putting them on the roof at the proper angle is to obtain more solar gain.

NEW STORAGE IDEAS

One of the problems of retrofitting a building with a solar window is the lack of storage mass. If you have a frame dwelling, you would not be likely to add concrete walls just to provide storage mass. If you have a masonry building, the interior is probably finished at least with wallboard of some sort. Two ideas for passive storage have been offered, either of which are adaptable to retrofit.

One idea suggests a ceiling tile that captures reflected light from the solar window, converts it to heat and stores the heat. The storage function is accomplished by a "phase change" material encapsulated in a polyester concrete ceiling tile. "Phase change" refers to the change of a material from a solid to a liquid, or from a liquid to a gas, or to the reverse of these changes. When a material goes through a phase change to a higher energy state, say from a solid to a liquid, it absorbs a great deal of heat. Then, when this material reverses its phase, as in returning from a liquid to a solid, it releases this "latent" heat. The material used in these ceiling tiles melts at 74 degrees. The solar window should have horizontal reflecting louvers similar to a venetian blind to direct the solar energy onto the ceiling.

Another idea, suggested by Dr. William Shurcliff of Harvard, places a bank of encapsulated phase change material in front of the solar window (the interior, of course). Solar energy is stored in the bank during the day and released at night. The bank can be placed in an enclosure that permits controlled release of the stored heat. One of the nice things about the heat bank idea is that it cuts down on the visible exposure of the room but still allows the entire window to be used for the collection and storage of heat. One of the objections to the solar window is glare, and another is excessive light intensity in the room. If the solar window were 7 feet high and the solar bank were 3 1/2 feet high, one-half of the glare and intensity would be eliminated without destroying any of the heat collecting properties. At one time it was common to see steam or hot water registers under a window, placed there to cut off the flow of cold air from the window. Another nice thing about the solar bank is that it should be a reminder of how things used to be, and, being familiar, should be aesthetically pleasing.

The problem with these phase change materials is that they tend to separate and lose their effectiveness after a large number of cycles. It has been found, however, that the life of the material can be greatly extended by encapsulating it in layers no more than one-quarter inch thick. The cells of the solar bank and the ceiling tile are capsules of this dimension. The ultimate life of the material with the new packaging is not known. Assuming that any installation you make ought to be good for 20 years, the material should be capable of cycling over 7000 times without deteriorating (figuring that it might undergo a phase change once every day winter and summer). Hopefully, by the time you get ready to apply this idea to your own solar window the life cycle problem will be solved. At least, you should be aware that experiment and brainstorming are going on to solve the problem of energy storage for retrofit of solar energy.

ACTIVE SOLAR SYSTEMS

There are two types of active systems, the air and the liquid, defined by the heat distribution fluid.

The active solar collector is housed in some sort of box of convenient dimension, say 4 × 8 feet. The important elements of the collector are an absorber plate made of copper, aluminum or steel, a special black or green absorber paint covering the surface of the absorber plate, insulation back of the plate to prevent loss of heat, and a transparent cover 2″ to 4″ above the plate to admit light and trap the heat.

In the liquid system, pipes are closely bonded to the absorber plate or made a part of the plate itself. The liquid in the pipes becomes hot by conduction from the absorber plate. The liquid circulates through the house by means of pumps, transferring the heat to the rooms or to the storage tank.

In the air system, the hot absorber plate heats the air between the plate and the cover. Fans in the distribution system blow the heated air either into the rooms or the storage bin.

The fluid in a liquid system is almost always water. Since water expands when it freezes, something must be done to prevent damage to the pipes. Sometimes an antifreeze is added to the water circulating in the pipes. In this case, a heat exchanger is needed inside the storage tank in order that all the water in the system need not be treated with antifreeze. Sometimes a draindown system is used, whereby water circulates in the collector pipes only when the sun has warmed the collector plate sufficiently to heat the water, and the water is retained in storage at other times. Sometimes the pipes are made of rubber, which is not damaged when the water inside freezes. Air collectors, of course, do not have to be protected from freezing.

Low iron clear glass and Kalwall fiberglass are the leading contenders for choice of cover plate material. Sometimes plastics such as Lexan are used. Sometimes Tedlar, a thin sheet plastic, is used as the second, or inner, cover.

There are pros and cons about whether one or two cover plates should be used. As you have already discovered in our discussion about windows, glass (and other materials that transmit light) has a low resistance to heat conduction. The air inside a collector becomes quite hot— perhaps to 150 degrees or more. From our heat loss equations we can easily see that, with the low resistance of glass and the high temperature difference (say, 20 degrees outside and 120 degrees inside), there is a lot of heat loss. A great amount of the heat converted inside the collector gets lost by conduction, especially if there is a strong wind blowing. One way to cut down the heat loss is, obviously, to use two cover plates, or two sheets of glass, as we do with windows.

But to do so reduces the light transmission through the cover. Cover plate material transmits less than 90% of the light striking it. A second cover plate reduces the transmittance to less than 80%. The energy available for conversion to heat drops. The cover plate in many cases is the most expensive part of the collector; two cover plates make the collector that much more expensive. Many solar engineers feel that, economically, the reduced heat loss does not pay for the cost of the extra cover plate and the lowered heat gain. One of the difficulties is that not enough study has been given to the effect of climate on the decision to use one or two cover plates. There should be trade-offs between cost of heat loss and degree days and average wind intensity.

Another component of the active solar system is the storage facility. For air systems, a rock bin is usually employed. River gravel or other stones about 2″ in diameter are customarily chosen. Fire brick or other ceramic or masonry material could as easily be selected, except for the cost. The object is to combine the maximum amount of mass with the maximum amount of surface exposure to the heated air plus the least resistance to passage of air through the mass. The disadvantage of rock storage is that, compared to water, it takes a much greater volume to store an equivalent amount of heat.

Water is customarily chosen as the storage medium for liquid systems. It is contained in an insulated concrete, steel or plastic tank located in the basement, or in a utility room of a slab floor. If there is no room in the house, it may be buried in the ground, provided waterproof insulation is used. Tank capacities of around 2000 gallons are usually specified for conventional installations. This capacity is enough to last 2 or 3 days without sunshine. Less than 1/2 this capacity would be required for the Ultra home.

We described the use of the property of "phase change" of certain materials (such as Glauber's salts) for passive storage. The latent heat of fusion acquired during the phase change greatly increases the storage capacity of a material; the storage capacity is a valuable property in a passive heating system because there is so little temperature difference to work with.

The greater capacity of phase change materials also makes them desirable for active system storage. In this case the extra capacity means that a much smaller storage volume is required. The container for phase change storage would be about 1/3 that of the required water tank.

We mentioned the objection to phase change salts: the number of cycles they can undergo seems to be limited. If someone tries to sell you a heat of fusion storage, make sure that he can give you an absolute 10 year guarantee and that he will be around in 10 years to honor it.

The heat from a liquid system is easier to distribute because the pipes are smaller than ducts and go around corners more easily. Liquid systems are easier to install in an established house, unless you already have a distribution system that can be used by the solar plant. Liquid systems often have problems with corrosion. Often there are two or three different kinds of metals among the distribution components; serious electrolysis problems can result unless special precautions are taken. Liquid systems also introduce many joints, each of which contribute to the possibility of leakage. There is no reason for corrosion or leakage to occur if competent people supply and install the equipment. In this young industry you cannot always be assured of this level of competence.

One of the more serious problems with liquid systems has to do with solenoid valves, not with the solar capabilities at all. Solenoid valves are operated by electricity, often with a magnetic plunger. When they shift there may be a loud and annoying "thump" unless properly selected and installed. Several electrically operated valves are necessary for automatic operation of a solar system.

Air systems have the advantages of less complexity and freedom from freeze-ups or corrosion. One big disadvantage is the need for a much larger storage container. Since rock has a much lower specific heat than water, it takes greater volume to store the same amount of heat. For new construction this problem is easy to solve. For retrofit it may not be so easy. Sometimes it requires a little ingenuity.

For example, perhaps you have a front porch badly in need of repairs. The floor boards and some of the beams have decayed. You've beeen thinking about doing an extensive repair job. If you are installing a solar system do not miss this opportunity to provide yourself with storage space. First talk with your solar engineer and get his ideas about how it should be done. Then, after you have torn down the old porch, build a tank whose perimeter is the dimensions of the porch. You can also dig down a few feet to get greater volume, if you wish. If you wish an air storage bin, fill the tank with stone and pour a concrete slab on top. The slab becomes the floor of your new porch. If you wish a water storage, you may use either a concrete top or a wooden porch floor as the cover, but you must leave a manhole to enable you to get into the tank sometimes. If your new porch is 8 feet wide and 10 feet long, and your tank is 3 feet deep, your storage capacity will be over 1700 gallons of water, which is more than enough for the size of solar installation we are recommending.

SOLAR EFFICIENCY

A word about efficiency is in order because, as soon as you begin to inquire about active systems, the vendors will praise the efficiency of their own product compared to others. You should be forewarned about the fact that there is some difficulty in defining what efficiency really means.

The question seems simple enough on the surface. Efficiency of a solar collector ought to mean the ratio of the amount of heat you can get out of a collector to the amount you put in. The amount you put in is the amount of solar energy falling on the face of the collector. The efficiency measured in the laboratory is a fair measure of the performance on the job, but not the only measure. It is coming to be common practice that all commercial collectors must be measured for efficiency in a testing laboratory to approved standards. The laboratory test measures the instantaneous, static, steady state efficiency of the collector. After the test set-up has reached a steady state condition, the technician measures the input and output and says that this ratio is the efficiency. The conditions of the job, however, are dynamic.

For example, there is the problem of response time, which is not often considered. The response time of a collector will have a lot to do with the amount of heat it can collect during short bursts of sunshine, as typically happens during a partly cloudy day. The collector plate cannot transfer heat until it has warmed up. If it is slow to warm up, not much heat is collected during short intervals of sunshine. On such a day the efficiency of one collector might be much different from another with a fast response time.

Then, of course, high efficiency of the collector does not necessarily mean high efficiency in the rest of the system. What counts for you is the ratio of the amount of heat you get into your home to the amount the sun supplies to the face of the collector. In fact, your most important efficiency ratio is the one that determines the lifetime cost, say 20 years, of the system per Btu. If the lifetime cost of the system amortized over 20 years, including interest, can supply you with heat for $5 or less per million Btu, you have a good buy. Good static efficiency, which the vendor will brag about, is necessary to achieve this long-term cost effectiveness, but it is not the only important feature of the system.

One of the interesting quirks of any solar collector is the fact that the lower the output temperature the higher the efficiency. One of the objectives of collector designers has been to try to raise the output temperature while maintaining high efficiency. Operating, or output, temperature can be controlled in system design by regulating the flow of the transfer fluids.

You should be aware that you can heat your home with a very small temperature difference between the source and the thermostat. We noted that passive systems can function on a 5 degree difference. All you need is a greater volume of transfer fluid movement. You can heat your home quite satisfactorily with a collector delivering 130 degree, or even 120 degree, fluid temperature. If you were building a new home, you could use a flat plate collector delivering 120 degrees, and it would be an advantage because the efficiency would be greater. For retrofit, the problem is a little different. You will probably want to couple the solar output into your existing distribution system, which has been designed to handle heat in the order of 150 degrees or more. You will not get satisfactory operation out of a 120 degree collector with such a delivery system. You will need to modify your distribution system or buy a collector capable of delivering higher temperatures. Engineering consists largely of finding the most profitable trade-offs and compromises, which is what you have to do in selecting a collector.

MORE IDEAS ABOUT HEAT

One concept of great importance to you provides an understanding of the relation between temperature and Btu's. One degree is one Btu difference in a pound of water. If all we ever had to deal with were pounds of water, then one degree would always equal one Btu. But virtually every substance absorbs less heat than water. Physicists relate the ''specific heat'' of all substances to that of water. If a substance has a specific heat of .5, it will rise .5 degree when absorbing one Btu. The low specific heat of rock is the reason why it takes a much larger volume of rock than of water to store the same amount of heat. If you really want to get into an understanding of solar heat, you need to look into ideas about specific heat.

Another important idea is that the amount of solar radiation received is a function of the area of surface and the angle of incidence. The sun irradiates a unit area of surface with just so much energy and no more. Some people have heard of solar furnaces that can reach 3000 degrees and wonder why it is not a simple matter to harness solar energy. But a solar furnace collects the energy from hundreds of square feet and focuses it onto a spot of maybe 10 square inches. There are the same number of Btu's in the 10 square inches at 3000 degrees as there are in the total area of the collector—actually somewhat fewer because we must recognize the efficiency of the furnace. So our roof collector of 200 square feet is working with the same number of Btu's regardless of whether it is delivering an output of 120 degrees, 150 degrees or 180 degrees. You just get a smaller volume of heating fluid at 180 degrees than at 120 degrees.

The function of angle of incidence is easy to understand in your own experience. You are aware that if the sun shines directly upon you, you get warmer than if it comes in from an angle.

If you can work with collector temperatures at a lower level, the total quantity of usable energy is greater than at a higher temperature due to the better efficiency. However, there are situations where the higher temperature is an economic and practical advantage. For example, you require less storage mass, or volume, at higher temperatures. Take the case of rock storage at 120 degrees and at 170 degrees, or at 50 and 100 degree differences from the thermostat. If the rock in use has a storage capacity of .2 Btu per pound per degree, it will require 1000 cubic feet to store 1 MBTU at 120 degrees but only 500 cubic feet to store the same amount at 170 degrees.

There are collectors able to reach 170 degrees and more quite easily. They are of various designs. Some have V-shaped grooves that concentrate 3 or 4 times as much area onto the bottom of the groove where the collector pipe is located. Some have semi-parabolic shaped sides to these grooves. Sometimes the collector pipe at the bottom of these grooves is pumped to a vacuum to lessen the conductance loss of heat. Sometimes the face of the groove is covered with a longitudinal Fresnel lens. Some of these collectors can produce outputs of 250 to 300 degrees.

One of the confusions that will beset you when you first look at solar collectors is the claims about temperature output. It will clarify your thinking if you recognize classes of temperature range and the purpose of each range. We like to think of three temperature ranges: low temperature to about 150 degrees for space heating; medium temperature from about 150 to just over 200 degrees; high temperature from about 212 to over 400 degrees for special process applications. Most of the good quality flat plate collectors can operate with pretty good efficiency up to 150 degrees. The concentrating collectors can operate over 200 degrees. Collectors that employ some variation of focusing can reach the higher temperatures.

Much of the motivation for research in the medium temperature range has been the desire to solve the air conditioning problem. No presently feasible and commercially available solar air conditioner will work with input temperatures less than about 180 degrees, and temperatures over 200 are desired for efficient operation. A number of quality collectors able to operate over 200 degrees are now available. The residential solar air conditioners now obtainable are for use only as central systems, and they are much more expensive than conventional equipment. The solar air conditioner that can compete with today's window unit is a long, long way off.

The significant point for us is that there is no reason for us to think of using anything other than the low temperature collector. High temperature systems might be a good answer to the storage problem, but researchers are hardly aware of the potential there. The degree of sophistication required for high temperature storage has not yet been approached. We have pointed out that space heating and storage at 120 degrees can be satisfactory. Quality low temperature collectors and system designers are available, if you choose them with care.

Hence, our suggestion: There is no need to wait for some wonderful technological discovery in solar equipment. These wonderful discoveries have already been made and have been brought to a high state of development. What is needed now is better marketing, better system engineering, better installation, responsible maintenance and meaningful guarantees. We need educated buyers who know how to define what they need. Perhaps by now you realize that, as an educated buyer, you need to know a lot about both solar energy and about energy efficient homes.

Contacts for solar heating information are: Owens-Corning Fiberglas, Fiberglass Tower, Toledo, OH 43659; National Mineral Wool Association, 382 Springfield Ave., Summit, NJ 07901; National Cellulose Insulation Manufacturers Association, 400 West Madison Street, Chicago, IL 60606; Insta-Foam Products, Inc., Joliet, IL 60435; and Olin Chemicals, 120 Long Ridge Road, Stamford, CT 06904 (foam insulation).

10

Can This Old House Be Saved?

Can my old house be upgraded to the Ultra class?

If you were building a new home, your designer and contractor would have to use all of the latest techniques in order to succed in building an Ultra class structure. It's not easy.

You may very well ask, "What chance do I have of turning my rambling old mansion into the self-sufficient model of the coming age?"

We define the Ultra home as one capable of supplying 100% of its own heat requirements during all but the worst three months of the year and about 80% of the requirements during these worst months. We expect the needs during these worst months to be so small that simple and inexpensive methods and sources of supplemental heat can be used. We expect this home not to require more than 200 square feet of active solar collector per thousand square feet of floor (perhaps up to 300 square feet in the most northern regions) to meet these design goals. We expect the collector to supply 100% of the domestic hot water needs of a family of four during the warm months and not less than 60% of the needs during the worst months. These criteria define the performance specifications that must be applied to energy efficiency and to solar gain. We have described here what these specifications are and how to meet them.

We suggest that by diligent effort, persistence and intelligent choices any house can be upgraded to meet these specifications and can thus join the Ultra class. If so, then your rambling old mansion can indeed be saved.

COMPARISONS

Let us work out some comparisons and see what the numbers tell us. Tables 10-1 and 10-2 summarize our findings. Table 10-1 deals with the numbers for a 4000 DD climate at 40 degrees latitude, and Table 10-2 deals with a 6500 DD climate at 48 degrees latitude. In the heat gain, HG, column of Table 10-1, we assume 50 square feet of solar window and 200 square feet of active collector. In Table 10-2, we assume 100 square feet of solar window and 200 square feet of active collector. We calculate the monthly heat loss for each climate for both the Superior and the Ultra class of FM home because we want to see how close we come to the criteria in both classes. We include domestic hot water (DHW) expenditures in both tables.

We assume that you will naturally include solar heated domestic hot water with your solar space heating system. Not only will it save money on another energy cost, but also the dollar per Btu for your solar system comes down if you can use the collector all year long.

Computing the DHW expenditure is easy. You assume 40 gallons of 120 degree water per person per day and a 4-member family. Multiply that answer by the number of days in a month. Assume that water from the mains is at 60 degrees in the fall and at 50 degrees in the winter. So the water has to be raised either 60 or 70 degrees. One gallon of water weighs 8.34 pounds. It therefore takes 8.34 Btu per degree to raise the water above the main temperature. The arithmetic, then, is:

$$40 \times 4 \times 8.34 \times da/mo \times 60 \text{ or } 70.$$

TABLE 10-1.   HEAT LOSS-HEAT GAIN BALANCE AT 4000 DD & 40° LATITUDE, MONTHLY MBTU

MONTHLY	HG	HL			BALANCE	
		Superior	Ultra	DHW	Superior	Ultra
Oct.	6.8	2.1	1.69	2.48	+2.2	+2.63
Nov.	6.3	3.93	2.04	2.4	+ .03	+1.86
Dec.	6.2	6.15	3.19	1.73	−1.68	+1.28
Jan.	6.5	6.66	3.46	1.73	−1.89	+1.31
Feb.	6.5	6.02	3.13	1.51	−1.03	+1.86
Mar.	7.2	5.29	2.75	2.89	− .98	+1.56
Apr.	6.5	3.29	1.71	2.4	+ .81	+2.39

The plus signs in the *Balance* column means that the solar window and active collector probably provide a surplus of energy during the month. The minus signs indicate a probable shortage from the solar sources during the month. Note that in this climate solar can probably provide 100% of the energy requirements of the Ultra class home during all months. The Superior class home almost meets our criteria for supplying all but 20% of the needs during Dec. and Jan. It does meet that criteria in Feb. and Mar. even though there is a shortage during those months. Remember that our criteria accept a reduction of the DHW specification to 60% of total self-sufficiency during the worst months.

TABLE 10-2. HEAT LOSS-HEAT GAIN BALANCE AT 6500 DD & 48° LATITUDE, MONTHLY MBTU

MONTHLY	HG	HL			BALANCE	
		Superior	Ultra	DHW	Superior	Ultra
Oct.	7.1	3.6	1.71	2.48	+1.03	+2.91
Nov.	6.1	6.73	3.2	2.40	−3.03	+ .50
Dec.	5.7	10.5	4.98	1.73	−6.53	−1.01
Jan.	6.1	11.39	5.41	1.73	−7.02	−1.04
Feb.	6.6	10.29	4.88	1.57	−5.26	+ .15
Mar.	7.7	8.87	4.21	2.89	−4.06	+ .60
Apr.	5.8	5.55	2.63	2.40	−2.15	+ .77

To comply with our criteria, we reduce the DHW expenditure to .60 for December, January and February in computing Tables 10-1 and 10-2.

Now look at the two tables and note a surprising discovery. You do not even need to go to the Ultra class to approach the ideal! You can come pretty close just by upgrading to the Superior class. In the 4000 DD climate the Superior home meets the criteria except for being about 5 MBTU short for the season and being short in March. The fossil fuel cost of 5 MBTU is $25. In the 6500 climate, the Superior home is short in all months but October. Even so, the back-up cost, probably from the already in place heating system, amounts to only about $125. If this home in the 6500 DD climate were in the Ultra class, its shortfall would only be a little over 1 MBTU per month for two months, December and January.

CONCLUSION

The conclusion is that you can save that old house if you can get a combination of around 300 square feet of solar window and active collector and can upgrade somewhat better than the Superior class in climates above 5000 DD.

We do not recommend going to less than 200 square feet of active collector because that amount will be necessary to give 100% solar DHW in the non-winter months. Nor do we recommend going much more than that amount, unless you find it impossible to put in solar windows. The exception is that up to 300 square feet of active collector seems to be advisable in climates above 8000 DD.

DECISIONS

Can you find any place in your home to put up 100 square feet of solar window? Even if you could, does it face south? If there is a sufficient area facing south, perhaps it looks into a part of the house that should not be heated or is far from the main living quarters.

You may face a similar problem with solar collectors. Perhaps the ridge pole of your home runs north and south. Apparently you have no place to put a collector.

But don't be too sure. Use your ingenuity. Read a lot of solar energy literature. Go to meetings. There are many, many ways to mount collectors. Nobody says collectors have to be placed on a south sloping roof. Just the collectors have to slope south. Nobody says collectors have to be laid out in a single array. Nobody says all the collectors on a home have to be of the same kind. Hang some here, some there. Mount some vertically on the side of the house. Use an air type on that odd-ball wing. Figure out the solar gains room by room, if you find it difficult to distribute heat or to treat the whole house as a unit. Do a lot of brainstorming. Talk with the experts every chance you get. Don't settle for the first idea that comes into your head. Wait until you get several ideas, and then choose the one that best fits your long-term goal. Don't count on the experts to lead you to your long-term goal. They will only solve bits and pieces. That is, be your own person, your own engineer. It boils down to the fact that only you can know your own goal and only you can figure out how to get there.

Perhaps your home is surrounded by trees. That one is easy to solve. You simply make a decision whether it is to be trees or solar energy. Perhaps the neighbor's trees interfere. Sun rights are a problem lawmakers will eventually have to solve. Until they do, perhaps you can strike up a bargain with your neighbor whereby you purchase the sun rights from him in exchange for his cutting down the offending trees.

Perhaps the problem is money. Money values are often psychological. We think nothing of spending more on an automobile than we would on a solar system, and then we proceed to wear it out in 2000 hours of driving. We would get more than 2000 hours of use out of a solar system in one winter.

Perhaps the solutions we have suggested are too simplified for application to a real situation. We have used a simple, no frills, rectangular, low-priced home as an example. We have dealt with a thousand square feet of floor space. But your home has 2500 square feet of space, and it rambles, and it has wings and dormers, and it has crazy gables, and its distribution of rooms is unusual. But if your problem is complex, simplify it by dealing with it in pieces. Again we say, if you can't treat your home as a unit, figure it out room by room.

Perhaps you live on the prairie where the scarcity of trees makes our recommended wood stove impractical. Consider the possibility of a windmill, which can produce electricity that can be turned into heat.

Our central proposition is revolutionary, but it is not especially original with us. Many competent solar engineers and architects have the same viewpoint. The conventional viewpoint, and the one assumed by almost all government energy planners, is that solar can—maybe—supply 30% to 50% of the load as a supplement. Our proposition is that by an application of intensive conservation solar can supply all but 10% to 20% of the load, and the back-up load is a supplement, not a primary source.

This proposition becomes revolutionary because the supplementary load is so modest it can be supplied by simple and self-dependent methods. In the Ultra home the supplement has to supply 10% to 20% of perhaps 25 MBTU. But conventional wisdom asks solar to supply 30% to 50% of perhaps 75, 125 or even 250 MBTU. Now, 20% of 25 MBTU is so modest it can be supplied by some simple device, such as a wood stove. Our proposition has become revolutionary when the home owner no longer has to depend on the factory system to pump energy into his home but can cut up his own wood. Or, if he prefers to have the factory pipe in what he does need, his requirements are so small he is not at the mercy of the suppliers.

Our central concept is usually applied to new construction. We hope we have pointed out how to apply it to the retrofit of established buildings.

More contacts are: Shawn Buckley, Dept. of Mechanical Engineering, Massachusetts Institute of Technology, Cambridge, MA 02139 (Buckley panels); *Solar Age*, monthly, 200 East Main St., Port Jervis, NY 12771; *Wood Burning Quarterly*, 8009 34th Avenue South, Minneapolis, MN 55420. In most places there are government energy centers available to provide information and assistance. There are also many local and regional solar energy associations. Watch your newspaper for news about them. We do not list makers of solar collectors and systems. There are too many of them, and they are easy for you to find.

Index